MW00582808

Triptych
and Iphigenia

Books by Edna O'Brien

The Country Girls

The Lonely Girl

Girls in Their Married Bliss

August Is a Wicked Month

Casualties of Peace

The Love Object and Other Stories

A Pagan Place

Zee & Co.

Night

A Scandalous Woman and Other Stories

Mother Ireland

I Hardly Knew You

Mrs. Reinhardt and Other Stories

A Rose in the Heart

Returning

A Fanatic Heart

The High Road

Lantern Slides

Time and Tide

House of Splendid Isolation

Down by the River

Wild Decembers

In the Forest

EDNA O'BRIEN

Triptych
and Iphigenia

Grove Press
New York

Iphigenia first published in 2003 Methuen Publishing Limited

FIRST EDITION

Printed in the United States of America
Published simultaneously in Canada

Library of Congress Cataloging-in-Publication Data
O'Brien, Edna.
    Triptych and Iphigenia / Edna O'Brien.—1st ed.
        p. cm.
    ISBN 0-8021-4154-4
    1. Women—Drama.   2. Mistresses—Drama.   3. Mothers and daughters—
Drama.   I. Title.
PR6065.B7T75 2004
822'.914—dc22   2004042381

Grove Press
an imprint of Grove/Atlantic, Inc.
841 Broadway
New York, NY 10003

05 06 07 08   10 9 8 7 6 5 4 3 2 1

For
Chris Smith

CONTENTS

TRIPTYCH

Triptych was first presented at Magic Theatre (Chris Smith, artistic director; David Gluck, managing director) in the Sam Shepard Theatre, Fort Mason Center, San Francisco, on December 6, 2003. The cast was as follows:

MISTRESS Lise Bruneau
WIFE Julia Brothers
DAUGHTER Tro M. Shaw

Director Paul Wentworth

Designer Kate Edmunds

Lighting Kurt Landisman

Costume Designer B. Modern

Sound Designer Michael Woody

Properties Artisan Sarah Ellen Joynt

Stage Manager Sabrina Kniffin

Production Manager Kenny Bell

Casting Director Jessica Heidt

MISTRESS, Clarissa

WIFE, Pauline

DAUGHTER, Brandy

The action takes place in New York City.

Downstage left—a white wrought iron bench.

Each character has her own space onstage but at times invades the space of the other.

MISTRESS*'s area—a staircase, a makeup table, a makeup case, a mirror with makeup lights, two shawls, and a book;* The Duchess of Malfi. *A long narrow window to the rear.*

WIFE*'s area—a glass-top table, a drinks tray, glasses, a silver cigarette box, a pack of tarot cards, unlit candles in various sconces, a white orchid in a pot, a china umbrella stand with a man's black umbrella.*

She is wearing a wraparound red skirt and a black sweater.

DAUGHTER*'s area—above wife's area. A futon. A small drum and set of drumsticks.*

She is wearing a miniskirt and different colored slides in her hair.

Music—Jimmy Durante:
When I fall in love
It will be for ever
Or I'll never
Fall in love
When I give my heart
It will be . . . for ever

Stage lighting comes on fully as MISTRESS *dressed in black as widowed Duchess of Malfi (circa 1601) stands before her mirror, saying her lines inaudibly. She is clearly nervous. On the bureau a vase of exquisite flowers.*

MISTRESS *(saying her lines)*   The misery of us, that are born great,
  We are forc'd to woo, because
  None dare woo us:
  And as a tyrant doubles with his words,
  And fearfully equivocates: so we
  Are forc'd to express our violent passions
  In riddles, and in dreams . . .

She stops suddenly as in the mirror she sees a hand come around the door, then a woman enter in dark glasses, wearing a long cream raincoat and carrying a large bunch of sunflowers.

WIFE   I hope you like sunflowers . . . not everybody's taste, of course . . . somewhat glaring . . . brazen, but I find them so . . . sturdy . . . the sunflower.

Triptych

MISTRESS I think you've come to the wrong dressing room.

WIFE (*ignoring that*) Il Girasole. On a train in Tuscany and Umbria one passes field after field of them . . . scorching, my honeymoon, our honeymoon was in pensions in Umbria . . . field after field of hot flowers . . . the bedrooms so cool . . . shutters drawn, dark brown furniture, dark brown fourposters . . . and the linen starched so stiff . . . it literally crunched when we lay on it . . . yes, the bedroom so cold and chaste and the fields so very hot and the lovers so ardent (*brusque*) not married, are you? . . . no little kids to grace the walls . . . a dressing room is quite a lonely place.

MISTRESS Who are you?

WIFE A stranger . . . just popped by to wish you well on your opening night and give you a flower . . . not at all as beautiful as those (*examining the flowers in the vase*) someone with more taste than moi . . . an admirer (*nostalgic*) it brings me back . . . how it brings me back . . . I was an actress, too . . . ingénue . . . I had a future, people compared me to some of the greats . . . then cupid struck in the form of a young man who just decided to hang around the stage door, pestering me, the way I am pestering you . . . just waltzed into my life.

MISTRESS I shall have to have you removed.

WIFE Not before I wish you well. I bet you're superstitious, especially on a night like this . . . all jitters.

MISTRESS How did you get in here?

WIFE The door was ajar. I walked in and walked down the stairs, simple. And now, I will vanish, like the sisters in that Scottish play, which we don't mention . . . Good luck, Duchess.

Woman puts down the flowers and goes.

Mistress picks up the flowers, then unnerved, throws them down.

VOICE OF STAGE MANAGER   Ladies and Gentlemen of the
Duchess of Malfi Company: Please take your places for the
top of the show. Places, please, for the top of the show.

*Mistress walks over the flowers and toward the stairs. She ascends
it holding up her costume.*

Lights go slowly down.

SCENE TWO

Darkness.

*Dulcimer music of the period is intermingled with a collage of lines
from* The Duchess of Malfi *as the wind rises and gathers to a
storm.*

*The vase of flowers overturns and the exquisite flowers fall to the
floor. All the flowers blow around the stage, up, down, and
around, omens of what is to come.*

Loud clapping offstage. Lights back on.

SCENE THREE

*Mistress, out of her costume, wears a kimono. The Wife has
returned.*

*Wife has the sleeves of her coat rolled up and is wearing elbow-
length black velvet gloves; she is clapping and smiling.*

WIFE   Bravo . . . Bravo. You were wonderful . . . wonderful
. . . I loved just before you were strangled when you said,

"Give my little boy some syrup for his cough." So beautiful . . .

MISTRESS (*crisp*)   Thank you.

WIFE   When is your birthday? . . . Wouldn't it be funny if we had the same birthday?

MISTRESS   Why would it be funny?

WIFE (*mock serious*)   Destiny.

MISTRESS (*holding the door open*)   If you will excuse me . . . I have friends waiting.

WIFE   Of course you have. (*theatrical*) Then I'll go pray; no, I'll go curse the stars.

Wife goes out.

MISTRESS   Jesus.

Mistress picks up the broken vase and some of the flowers.

The telephone rings and she jumps, then goes tentatively to answer it. As she listens her expression changes to a smile.

MISTRESS   Yes, of course I know . . . How do I know? . . . Henry . . . I can't see you . . . I cannot. (*She listens, her smile happier.*) You know very well why . . . you are a married man and I have been down that road before. (*emphatic*) It's hell. What's hell about it?—when the married man goes home. Of course I want to . . . (*whisper*) you know that. (*anxious*) There's been a crazy woman in here . . . it's been a very crazy night . . . storm . . . oh, it went well . . . so they say . . . thank you for the exquisite flowers . . . by the way, I thought you were in the country . . . you what? . . . (*She cradles the phone between mouth and ear.*) All right then . . . just

one drink . . . one night cap . . . promise . . . promise . . . I
have to do an interview tomorrow morning and *you* are not
a free man.

SCENE FOUR

Lights crossfade to bright light in Wife's area.

Very loud blues music—Billie Holiday, Aretha Franklin.

*Wife is a little drunk as she dances and sings to the music. She is
wearing a sleeveless vest and a very short skirt. She veers from
anger to false cheer, sometimes dancing, skipping the songs as her
mood and temper alter. At times she talks back to the music.*

WIFE (*mimicking the Mistress*) "I think you've come to the
wrong dressing room . . . If you will excuse me, I have
friends waiting."

BRANDY, *her daughter, enters, wearing a miniskirt and bright
socks.*

DAUGHTER Partying! All by yourself . . . Poor Mommy.

WIFE You look ridiculous.

DAUGHTER This one must be something . . . what does she
do? Cat-walk?

WIFE She's an actress.

DAUGHTER Famous?

WIFE Look Brandy, you've got to stand by me. You've got
to say, "Don't do it, Daddy . . . don't, don't do it."

DAUGHTER (*angry*) I hate this fucking house . . . scenes,
fights, tears . . . Daddy can't stand it . . . that's why he goes

to the country. . . . He can't work with a crazy woman like you.

WIFE (*quietly*) Brandy. I need you. You have got to stand by me in this . . . it's for everyone's sake.

DAUGHTER What's so different about her?

WIFE She'll play one of his heroines—a slut.

DAUGHTER You're nuts.

Daughter goes into her own area.

SCENE FIVE

On a board, pinups of her favorite rock stars and her father. She kisses her father's face.

DAUGHTER Silly Daddy . . . silly silly Daddy, (*scolding voice*) I'm watching you.

Daughter begins to pin the sheet to the wall.

DAUGHTER All my friends adore him . . . Two of them have crushes on him . . . They ask for his autograph because he's quite famous . . . he comes to school on opening day with my mother, my mother wearing stupid clothes and clunky jewelry . . . of course I prefer him . . . One Christmas Eve it was snowing and he lifted me out of bed and said (*conspiratorial voice*), "Would you like to see the tree in Rockefeller Center?" and he put Mummy's fur coat over me and we snuck out and got into a cab . . . it was magic, the tree, the lights, the snow, couples ice-skating after midnight, and my father holding me in a long fur coat, and people looking at us as if we were lovers. Yes, lovers.

Scene Six

Early morning. Light in Mistress's area. She is wearing jeans, hair tossed, bemused.

MISTRESS Oh God, oh God, oh God . . . I did show some gumption . . . at first, but then his hand, his thief's hand, came under my skirt and he said, "You could not have put those stockings and those garters on just to go straight home," and I said, "You could be right, Henry, you could be right."

Wife in Daughter's area.

Daughter reading a magazine interview.

DAUGHTER Actress tells why she takes on difficult roles.

WIFE *(brisk)* Go on.

DAUGHTER *(scanning)* Her deep entreating voice, her tragic heroines . . . *(skipping)* "Oriental fury," the pathos of a disappointed queen . . .

WIFE Her years.

DAUGHTER Doesn't say.

WIFE 'Course it doesn't say. *(intent voice)* A long lock of her hair.

DAUGHTER Not the voodoo crap that the maid did with snake oil and chicken's blood.

WIFE Yes, the voodoo crap with snake oil and cockerel's blood.

DAUGHTER *(cutting in)* It's ghoulish.

WIFE It worked on her husband.

DAUGHTER   He got run over.

WIFE   He had it coming. (*sweeter voice*) O, my precious snake oil and warm cockerel's blood, unhair her head, dim her eyes (*vicious*) . . . This malefaction must be stopped . . . a cuckoo in our nest.

DAUGHTER   I hate it when you act.

WIFE   Make her dull of tongue and dwarfish . . . a poor pastiche of what she was . . .

DAUGHTER   You should put yourself up for auditions . . . bit parts . . .

WIFE   This is not acting . . . feel my pulse . . . the man's gone mad . . . Her gypsy's lust.

Mistress takes up the story.

MISTRESS   (*on the floor or stretched on staircase*)   Your hair . . . your hair . . . kept going on about my hair . . . We mustn't fall in love, I said . . . speak for yourself, he said . . . Ran his forehead all along the wall . . . (*imitating Henry*) I am dying, Egypt . . . dying. It was there, no, not there. There. (*She kisses the wall.*) Anyone could have come in; says to expect him at all hours, he'll get a stepladder, bribe the man at the stage door, (*rueful*) I am dying, Egypt . . . dying.

Wife has come across to eavesdrop.

DAUGHTER   (*calls across*)   Mummy. What is love?

WIFE   Ask your father. Ask his whore.

SCENE SEVEN

Mistress comes downstage, sits on bench. Wife watches pantherlike and follows.

WIFE Ah, there you are.

MISTRESS So you must be Pauline.

WIFE Yes. I must be Pauline.

Wife sits.

Mistress moves along to distance herself

WIFE You have cats? (*waits*) You look like a cat person, a silver-haired or a tortoiseshell curled up on your lap . . . we have a dog, an old lazy setter—Jesse—getting on . . . oh yes, dozes most of the day.

MISTRESS I came here to be by myself.

Pause.

WIFE Ever pick anyone up on a park bench?

MISTRESS No.

WIFE I did. A Latino . . . I recognized him from our deli . . . we got chatting . . . he said he could cover a woman's face, any woman's face, with a paper bag, and he could tell her exact age from just feeling her cunt . . . A bit like telling the age of a tree from the circles in the trunk.

MISTRESS Not quite.

WIFE That got you going . . . I often wonder about women coming . . . us . . . us coming . . . if it's different for each one of our little individual cunty selves . . . men are so reserved about it . . . take you, now . . . you have this

15

composure . . . this veneer . . . Grace Kelly would play you
if you were ever to be played and if she were still alive . . .
but that's beside the point . . . as a matter of fact I would say
in the flagrante department you would crow as loud as the
rest of us.

MISTRESS You do rattle on . . . is it your nerves?

WIFE *(with a husky laugh)* No, sister. The one thing I take
care of, is the upstairs department. I mean life and love and
kids and all that stuff can send a woman loopy . . . I've seen
them . . . beautiful women . . . all bloated . . . out to lunch
with big hats and dark glasses because their husbands have
wandered . . . Do you know the surest way to keep your
man happy?

MISTRESS You are about to tell me.

WIFE Give him rope . . . be mysterious . . . tell him about
the Latino and the paper bag but don't say you met him on
a park bench . . . It was overheard. Every sensitive man
loves two women—Mamma Mia and Mamma Whore and
he's sincere about it . . . so let's not bitch about them . . . I
love men and I can see you love men unreservedly.

MISTRESS And how do you arrive at that conclusion?

WIFE Your swallow, *(pause)* the way you give little gasps,
little intakes, when that Duke, whatever the fuck his name
is, comes on to you in the play.

MISTRESS I am inhabiting the character, the Duchess of Malfi
. . . We are different creatures. My dear woman, how little
you know about the theater . . .

WIFE I know plenty. At this moment you are shit scared.

MISTRESS Why should I be shit scared?

WIFE Because you made a wrong connection, schmuck. You ate of the forbidden fruit. I want my husband, every last little piece of him.

MISTRESS Of course you do.

WIFE Let me tell you a cautionary story . . . one of his ex-whores sent him a list at Christmas, a list of what she wanted . . . Krug champagne, claret, Sèvres china . . . A French harlot . . . and at the very bottom she put in large capitals "A BABY."

MISTRESS I don't need a baby, thank you very much.

WIFE Aren't you curious to know how I found out about you, your existence, your invasion of my home? Dishes. He had actually washed up, he who never washed a cup in his life, and I said "You've had some whore in here, in my house . . ." I could smell you . . . he denied it of course . . . some big spiel about reading in a magazine on how to be a better husband (*bossy*) remember to wash up . . . buy flowers . . . don't forget her birthday, etc. . . . (*gleeful*) and I let him have it and we had one of our feisty fights and then we fucked (*pause*) not too long after you and he had fucked . . . something . . . some guardian angel told me to come back early from the country . . . so you better know what you are letting yourself in for . . . women, women throw themselves at him and I am always there in the ring for the last round.

MISTRESS I have no intention of throwing myself at anyone.

WIFE Oh yes you have. I found the note in his pocket (*mock sensitive*) "Please let us not fall in love, my darling" (*tough voice*) which signifies that you already have. What did you fall in love with . . . his mind, his cock, his graying temples, his fame?

MISTRESS (*curt*)   His shoes actually.

WIFE   Ha, ha, ha. His fancy shoes . . . they're so goddamn lecherous . . . the swank shoes for the swanky man. And he fell for your eyes, your beautiful cat-green eyes.

MISTRESS   They were contact lenses actually.

WIFE   Yes, but to him they were still the most beautiful cat-green contact-lens eyes, as he put it.

MISTRESS (*taken aback*)   He told you that?

WIFE   Of course. What he doesn't tell me I squeeze out of him . . . I suck it out of him like a shaman sucking a boil. They're all weak . . . and his repertoire when smitten isn't that original . . . , haven't you noticed that? . . . how many times have you been in love, Clarissa?

MISTRESS   Henry says I've never been in love before . . . I've been waiting for him.

WIFE   His favorite opening gambit.

MISTRESS   Three times actually.

WIFE   I am faithful to Henry but that does not mean that I do not have my little *amusements* . . . it also doesn't mean that I don't know how to make him jealous . . . he's wildly jealous . . . he's even jealous of my shrink, me lying down in a shaded room, telling a total stranger my fantasies; (*scolding*) I am friends with many of his exes (*laughs*) even while knowing that he goes back for the odd poke . . . I'm on a first-name basis with all of them . . . they've made calls in the middle of the night . . . I've made calls in the middle of the night . . . they've threatened to slit their wrists . . . (*quiet*) me too . . . so little variation in these messes . . . all that remains is the biannual fuck and debris.

Mistress gets up.

MISTRESS   I shall not be calling in the middle of the night or slitting my wrists . . . or . . .

WIFE   Oh yes, you will . . . When the heat's off, when he's quiet after he's come—introspective whereas once he was rapturous, you'll teeter, you'll lose your poise, you'll call in the middle of the night, *sobbing,* and you'll hang up, but he'll know it was you and I'll know it was you, we'll both know it was you and we'll snuggle up to each other in the dark, man and wife against the enemy outside.

Scene Eight

Lights come up on Daughter who is sitting by the drums but not playing.

DAUGHTER   She asked me to work on him. He came in here all sheepish and said "You have something to tell me, Brandy." It was awful. Then I blurted it out. I said, "Daddy, you're not to leave us ever." And he swore he wouldn't, couldn't. He was drinking a martini and let me take a couple of sips. We sat and talked. He said we'd go to Ireland in the summer and hire a horse and caravan and travel all over, like gypsies. His dad's people were from there, some big cloud over his dad . . . he kinda vanished, and his mom never got over it. . . . "What is love, Daddy?" I asked. . . . "Clarissa is one of us," and I could tell by the way he said her name that he was crazy about her, crazy about her. *(confidential)* I wanted to tell him, to swear to him that no man would ever come between him and me . . . it's something he should know . . . and he will.

MISTRESS (*declarative*) "Let's call it off, Henry, before we go in too deep," and he said we had gone in too deep. I asked him, was it Brandy? He said yes, that she was the closest thing in the world to him . . . in fact . . . he went so far as to say that if anything happened to her he could not go on living.

WIFE He confessed everything . . . where he saw you . . . why he got trapped . . . you playing the helpless maiden so convincingly . . . he broke down in my lap and said how sorry he was and I said I knew all along but kept it from him and he said, "God bless you for saying that," and then we both said, "Where do we go now?" and I said, "Let's stick together" . . . so we're going away . . . far, far away . . . he's going to write . . . he's going to write you out of his system . . . you'll be a memory . . . then you'll be a figure on a page.

MISTRESS Thank you, Pauline, for letting me know . . . in fact, he told me himself and we parted the best of friends.

DAUGHTER I might as well have been an orphan . . . Scooting off to Spain to make their marriage work and me here with Fatima, who doesn't speak a word of English . . . "You can have your friends over on weekends," Mommy said . . . I'll have my friends over . . . I'll wear her clothes . . . I'll sleep in their bed . . .

SCENE NINE

Mistress, Wife, and Daughter walk around the stage, breaking into each other's space and into each other's lines, talking in rapid urgent voices as the mood befits them.

WIFE The villa was not on the sea but up a long winding goat track.

MISTRESS   Manhattan was all mine. He was gone. I had an admirer, a Greek . . . took me to Greek restaurants and taught me Greek sayings.

WIFE   Henry wrote ten hours a day. I cooked delicious meals, left them on a tray outside his door . . . he was very quiet and very grateful.

DAUGHTER   Mummy writing to say how lovely the villa . . . how lovely the morning glory . . . the donkeys . . . bullshit.

MISTRESS   After the Greek left town there was a Scandinavian . . . he made fondue on his roof terrace . . . I got a taste for aqua vitae. "Skoal, Henry, skoal."

WIFE   One night we got very drunk together—

MISTRESS   Skoal, Henry, skoal.

WIFE   . . . very . . .

MISTRESS   . . . very . . .

WIFE & MISTRESS   . . . drunk.

WIFE   We danced and smooched . . . then we crawled into a washhouse and we made love . . .

MISTRESS   . . . and we made love . . .

WIFE   Afterward I cried . . .

MISTRESS   . . . and he said, "Why are you crying, darling?"

WIFE   And I said, "Do you know how long it is since we've made love?" And he said . . . "Don't, darling, don't."

DAUGHTER   Daddy sent a card every other day, telling me what a champ I was.

WIFE   We did not discuss his play . . . I suppose he knew that I knew she was in it . . . her ghost.

MISTRESS My acting got better . . . I did have one relapse . . . I was with friends upstate and a woman read the tea leaves and said that I was soon to be married . . . I snapped at her.

DAUGHTER I flew over to Spain for Easter . . . goats, donkeys, mules . . . miles off the beaten track . . . my mother did nothing but cook . . . she had a range of Escoffier cookbooks lined up.

MISTRESS (*enthralled*) I met a young man, not Greek, not Scandinavian: Jonathan, and he was English . . . perfect, perfect, he would come to almost every show and afterward he would give me a hug.

DAUGHTER Daddy said he wanted to read us the first act of his play. Mommy lit candles and got the drinks tray out and it was dire . . . it just dragged and dragged . . . I could see my mother twitching and then Daddy said, "What did you think of it?" and she gushed and he said, "For fuck's sake stop acting the little wife, Pauline."

MISTRESS He was all the things a lover should be. We were so happy, we rode bicycles around Central Park, we flew to Arizona to see an eclipse of the sun.

DAUGHTER The morning I was leaving Daddy broke off a flower and said, "Take that back to New York." So he was still hot for her.

WIFE I knew that his writing was at a standstill . . . We should never have gone there.

MISTRESS . . . mates, soul mates, we proposed to one another in the very same breath.

WIFE I got the blues. I went to the local doctor to see if he could give me something . . . The moment I laid eyes on him I forgot about the blues . . . there he was looking at me with his long El Greco face and his soft gray eyes . . . (*chuckling*) "I've never had to fake orgasm," I said. He almost fell off his chair.

MISTRESS Jonathan went back to England. The plan was that I would follow. How I missed him. How I missed him. I wore a sweater of his in bed, things like that.

WIFE El Greco got more and more excited and he said there were many women patients who would give anything to be in my boots or in my bed. He was looking at me quite longingly. I know that look. I've seen it on my husband's puss many a time.

MISTRESS I kept changing the dates for our wedding . . .

DAUGHTER When I got back, we cooked this fancy meal, Fatima and I, Mexican stuff; only three of my friends showed up, Betsy and Kim and Venus . . . No boys . . . Said they got lost . . . Someone gave them smack . . . And they couldn't keep track of the program. Daddy wrote and told me that my prince was waiting in the wings. Yeah, right.

MISTRESS One night I rang Henry's apartment . . . Why did I do it? God, the relief when nobody answered.

WIFE Not too long after, I twisted my ankle and Henry had to send for El Greco. He arrived rather late and he came into the bedroom and Henry left us alone. He drew off my sock or rather Henry's green sock and flung it away and looked at me with that, that . . . He *had* me in that room in those few stolen moments and I thought: We're even now, Henry and me . . . we're even and I can go down to that clinic anytime that I choose and have fingers stuck up into me . . . doctor's fingers stuck up into me. (*She claps her hands forcefully.*) I was wrong. Two mornings later Henry announced that we were going home.

They each return to their own area.

SCENE TEN

As Mistress enters her dressing room the phone is ringing. Her mirror lights come on as she answers it.

MISTRESS   Oh! . . . Buenos dias or Buenas noches or whatever they say . . . how was Spain . . . I don't need a present . . . I have everything I want . . . a what (*laughing*) a washboard . . . what do you think I am . . . a scrubber. I've got a wonderful part . . . guess. Well she's a girl who goes into the forest with her father who has been banished and she becomes a boy in order to chastise lovers . . . love is merely a madness . . . deserves a dark horse and a whipping . . . jealous . . . I've no need to be jealous, I'm getting married . . . he's called Jonathan and he's a forester and he has nothing to do with writing . . . with theater . . . an earth man.

She laughs heartily. He has put down the phone.

She takes one of her stage props and goes toward the stairs, reveling in her triumph.

She dons a shawl and walks all around the stage, triumphant.

MISTRESS   He was in the third row . . . watching, watching, and then just before the end he got up and he was here pleading, his arms out to lift me, to lift me down . . . he asked if Jonathan called himself Jon for short and then he took hold of my ribs and he mashed them and he said "You know fucking well that with me and you it's not acting, it's not theater, it's not writing, it's not forestry, and it's not Jonathan, and it's not false . . . the thing I'd waited half a year for . . . crushed my ribs so badly . . . I had to wear a . . . truss . . . this dressing room became our castle . . . he would leave things, his notebook, his cigarettes, his scarf, ribs of his hair. (*contrite*) Poor Jonathan.

SCENE ELEVEN

Action changes to Wife's area, which is in darkness.

A crash as Wife falls and various things fall off the table onto the floor.

Daughter comes in and turns on a light.

DAUGHTER Mommy! Oh shit.

WIFE He's seeing her again.

DAUGHTER Are you OK?

WIFE I don't know . . . I don't care.

Daughter starts to help her up.

DAUGHTER He'll get tired of her; he always does.

WIFE He's moved out some of his belongings . . . he's planning to leave us.

DAUGHTER So . . . we'll have to get used to it . . . other women do.

WIFE I'm not other women . . . he's my life . . . my rock . . . I'd rather he died than lose him to her.

DAUGHTER   That's sick.

WIFE   Show me a bit of kindness for once in your life . . . I know what you say about me . . . you and your friends . . . I'm stupid and I talk too much and I have no dress sense, none.

DAUGHTER   You're imagining it.

WIFE (*confidentially*)   I'll tell you something Brandy that I've never told you before . . . I was glad that you were a daughter . . . because if you were a son he'd be more jealous . . . mothers and their sons have this thing.

DAUGHTER   Thanks a bundle.

WIFE (*contrite*)   Brandy, we were so happy . . . we were so right for each other . . . we were inseparable . . . it was like a hand in a glove . . . I was the glove and he was the hand and then he was the glove and I was the hand. Oh, he changed slowly but surely . . . he changed. Fame, women . . . women idolizing him, in restaurants coming up to him and telling him how great he was . . . Henry, so reticent. (*tenderly*) Small things like the way his hair falls down over his face.

Daughter gets her up and sits her on a chair, comforting her.

DAUGHTER (*melting*)   Oh, Mommy.

WIFE (*sobbing*)   Brandy, pray that she dies.

Triptych

SCENE TWELVE

Light on Mistress's dressing room.

Mistress looks up to see Brandy wearing a tight-fitting velvet jacket with baseball cap.

MISTRESS   Hello Brandy . . . would you like a drink?

DAUGHTER   Stoli.

MISTRESS   Huh . . . you drink Stoli?

DAUGHTER   For fuck's sake don't you treat me like a child.

MISTRESS   OK. I won't.

DAUGHTER   You've got to give him up.

MISTRESS   Why?

DAUGHTER   It's harming his work.

MISTRESS   Does he know you're here?

DAUGHTER   Maybe. Maybe not.

MISTRESS   Does your mother know?

DAUGHTER   I tell her nothing.

MISTRESS   We have tried giving each other up, but it's no use . . . we are (*pause*) inseparable.

DAUGHTER   Bullshit.

MISTRESS   It may be bullshit to you but not to me.

DAUGHTER   And what about us . . . You haven't even given us a thought.

MISTRESS I have given you a thought . . . in fact I often walk past your building and I wonder what's going on up there, on the tenth floor.

DAUGHTER (*hitting her*) Mayhem. All for a fuck.

MISTRESS (*fends her off*) Young lady, there are things you have yet to learn . . . manners for one thing and propriety for another.

DAUGHTER You should hear my mother sobbing . . . it's like Niagara Falls.

MISTRESS Please don't.

DAUGHTER There are times when he has to pick her up and hold her and rock her in his arms like a baby . . . then he's in his office, on the phone to you, cooing.

MISTRESS Yes. Lovebirds.

DAUGHTER When she can't sleep she goes downstairs, wakens Jesse to play with a ball . . . back and forth, back and forth . . . all Jesse wants is to sleep. She's my dog, she followed me home from the subway last Christmas. She's the one I talk to, not them.

MISTRESS Surely that's not true.

DAUGHTER They're too wrapped up in themselves, they've no time for me . . . well, not enough time.

MISTRESS What do you want to be . . . ?

DAUGHTER A drummer.

MISTRESS Do you have a beau?

DAUGHTER Yeah . . . lots . . . but they're all geeks. Morons. I can talk to my father about movies or rock or hip-hop, or clothes, or my grades, or anything.

Pause.

MISTRESS   I would give him up, but I can't. He's part of my life now.

DAUGHTER (*angry again*)   Do you do it on the floor? Or on the stairs?

MISTRESS   Both.

DAUGHTER   We have suppers alone, together. He asks my advice. I tell him that it would be better if he went away . . . but really away . . . far away from the two of you . . . not upstate . . . not out west . . . but to another country altogether, and he says, "You're right . . . I should go far away because I haven't made anyone happy and I haven't done what I want to do."

Pause.

DAUGHTER   I love him.

MISTRESS   We each love him.

DAUGHTER   But I am his princess.

MISTRESS   So why be so jealous?

DAUGHTER (*with relish*)   I hate you. I stick pins all over your face every time I see a photograph of you . . . that simper, that Mona Lisa smile . . . I cut it out and paint a horrible black mustache on you and pin it up on my board. He's seen it. I read in the gossip column that you drink green tea all day and then champagne in the evening . . . champagne made from the white grape only.

MISTRESS   Bullshit.

DAUGHTER (*shouting*)   Go back to where you came from. . . . Leave . . . us . . . alone.

MISTRESS   I'm afraid I have to ask you to go.

Daughter leaves.

MISTRESS (*turning*)   Little did she know that she was to have a brother or a sister or a half brother or a half sister before long.

STAGE MANAGER (*offstage*)   Ladies and Gentleman of the As You Like It Company, this is your fifteen-minute call. Fifteen minutes, please.

SCENE THIRTEEN

Daughter watches as Wife starts to dress herself, preparing to go out. Mistress starts to dress herself for her part as Rosalind.

MISTRESS   I was out and about doing errands and a taxi stopped at the light and he opened the door and I got in and he said, "Where shall we go?" "North," I said and he tapped on the glass and told the driver to keep going north. Should I tell him or should I not. No one knew, certainly not Rosalind, she would scold me. (*clasps her waist*) He'll know soon enough . . . so will Rosalind in her doublet and hose.

DAUGHTER   We looked at places for Daddy to rent, so he could get down to his writing . . . one on the East River was quite something. I said "It will give you inspiration" and he gave me that gorgeous grin of his.

WIFE   What is this nonsense about renting an office . . . Complete waste of money.

MISTRESS   We came to a small town with dinky little houses and a pond; pairs of swans gliding by. After we'd checked in

at the inn, we sat in the bar and had champagne cocktails
. . . I'd never known him so open, so tender . . . said he'd
been dreaming a lot of his early life and how I came into it
. . . I was there in that place where I've never set foot.

WIFE I have a good idea—darling, we can turn the music
room into an office . . . it's never used. I'll put a minifridge
in, (*half scolding*) so you can mix your martinis.

DAUGHTER I begged him to take it . . . I could go after
school with my friends and sit around talking to Daddy . . .
listening to Daddy . . . telling stories.

MISTRESS His mother . . . his beautiful, high-strung mother
adoring him, everybody adoring him . . . he felt he didn't
have enough love to give back . . . what he preferred was
the fishing trips with his father in the mountains . . . two
men barely speaking a word and cooking supper on an open
fire at night.

WIFE Didn't tell you I had lunch with your publisher . . .
they're waiting with baited breath . . . he's a wine buff.

MISTRESS "Let the caged bird mate with the caged and the
wild bird male with the wild . . ." It came into my head and
I just spurted it out. "Which were we?" I asked him.

WIFE (*turning to Brandy*) You just stop calling real estate
people . . .

DAUGHTER (*cutting in*) Who says I'm calling real estate
people?

WIFE Three different firms called and I said we are not
interested in leasing property at the moment.

DAUGHTER (*bridling*) Without speaking to Daddy or me.

WIFE You're getting too big for your britches . . . you need
your butt kicked.

Mistress, swashing male attire as Rosalind, is by her mirror.

MISTRESS   He said we were swans, because swans mate for life. (*her hands on her waist*) When I tell him . . . will I lose him . . . Will it send him running . . . It couldn't, it can't. (*pause*) One word he said that keeps haunting me— *entrapment.* He dreaded entrapment.

STAGE MANAGER (v.o.)   As You Like It company: Please take your places for the top of the show. Places, please, for the top of the show.

Mistress goes toward stairs.

Wife walks past Daughter with scorn.

DAUGHTER   Off to get sloshed again?

WIFE (*oversweet smile*)   Noo.

Wife goes out.

Daughter looks after her, wrinkles her nose in mockery, then looks puzzled, goes out.

SCENE FOURTEEN

Mistress is onstage as Rosalind, relishing her role.

MISTRESS (*as Rosalind, playful*)   And in this manner . . . He was to imagine me his love, his mistress; and I set him every day to woo me.

Wife comes down the auditorium aisle, shouting.

WIFE   Whore . . . English whore.

Mistress continues as if she has not heard it.

MISTRESS (*as Rosalind*)   At which time would I, being but a moonish youth, grieve.

WIFE   Grieve and give him up . . . He's mine, mine.

MISTRESS (*as Rosalind, her voice getting rapider*)   . . . Be effeminate, changeable, longing and liking, proud, fantastical, apish, shallow, inconstant, full of tears, full of smiles.

WIFE   . . . full of treachery and deceit (*to audience*). Be not misled by these dulcet tones . . . she strews in her path desolation.

VOICES   Sssh . . . sssh. . . . sssh . . . sssh.

WIFE   We were a happy close-knit family until this well-bred whore entered our lives, broke us up . . . ruined us.

MISTRESS (*as Rosalind*)   For every passion something . . . something.

WIFE (*cutting in*)   Yes lady, an eye for an eye and a tooth for a tooth, every second of happiness you have stolen from me.

MISTRESS (*as Rosalind, misses a line*)   . . . would now like him, now loathe him, then entertain him, their forswear him, now weep for him, then spit at him.

Wife has climbed onto the stage.

Mistress endeavors to keep within her role.

MISTRESS (*as Rosalind, faltering*)   That I drave my suitor from his, from his mad humor of . . .

Daughter comes on stage and drags her Mother off.

DAUGHTER   You're so goddam dumb . . . so fucking stupid.

MISTRESS (*as Rosalind*)   . . . his mad humor of love to a living humor of madness . . . that I, that I drove my suitor from his mad humor of love to a living humor of that I, that I . . . that I . . .

She stops suddenly.

Her face freezes.

Lights go dark.

Lights come up on, wife in living room.

SCENE FIFTEEN

The next day.

Light up on Daughter reading a newspaper.

DAUGHTER   "Disturbance in theater brings giggles."

Wife takes the paper and tears it methodically and violently.

Conversation over her action.

DAUGHTER   He'll know.

WIFE   You can't tell him.

DAUGHTER   She'll tell him.

WIFE   She won't.

DAUGHTER   Why did you do it? Why did you make such an ass of yourself?

WIFE   I'll do anything.

Daughter goes to her own area, pulls up her skirt, tries on saucy garters, singing "It's a Man's World."

DAUGHTER   I slept over at Judy's house and we would all lie on her big bed and watch TV—Nancy, Venus, Betsy, and Kim, and me. That's how I met Nathan . . . He was really cute, except for his armpits. Judy's parents were so rich that they were never in any one place for more than twenty-four hours. Nathan would take turns sitting between the girls in his boxer shorts, said it was good for us to have the male energy lines, a helluva hip guy, I'll give him credit for that. . . . One night he brought a porno, people doing it nonstop, like a zoo . . . We couldn't stop guzzling the booze and giggling . . . Nathan gave himself a body scrub in the shower.

Mistress is sitting on the last step of the staircase.

MISTRESS (*low with emotion*)   When I told him, he froze. He said, "You've got to get rid of it." And I said, "No, it's mine, mine . . . I'll rear it alone." I've never seen a man so thrown, so flabbergasted, he went ashen. I said, "Is it your wife . . . is it your daughter?" and he said a most cutting thing. He said, "It's not my wife, it's not my daughter, it's you and it's me . . . A man thinks he has found a new woman, a great woman, but it always turns out to be the same bloody woman in different costume." He walked out of the restaurant; "You rat, you fucking rat!" I shouted and I was certain that he had merely gone down the street to think things over, men are wont to go down the street to think things over, but I was wrong. Not long after, I rang my friend Rachel to ask for her doctor's number and I took two weeks off work and learnt that my understudy was a wow.

Daughter lying on her futon, flicking through salacious magazines, whistles, etc.

DAUGHTER Wow, she's curvy . . . You've got a very big bush, madam, you could sweep Amsterdam Avenue with that.

SCENE SIXTEEN

Wife in raincoat and red beret approaches the Mistress's space pointing the ferule of the long black umbrella. She is smiling, almost laughing. She has had a few drinks, weaves a little.

WIFE (*singing*) Oh show me the way to the next whiskey bar
Oh pretty boy
Please don't ask why,
You know that you must die . . .
Oh, pretty boy

MISTRESS Whenever I saw a mother and a baby on the street I just burst into tears.

WIFE (*quizzical*) Your hair . . . something different . . . Seems shorter . . . Not quite so tousled.

MISTRESS You've been on the town, I see.

Wife, ignoring that, takes a photograph out of her wallet.

WIFE Souvenir. Thought you'd like to see what Henry looked like when we met twenty years ago . . . He'd seen a postcard of James Dean wearing a cap, standing by some fence so he got himself the same cap. From the moment I met him I decided that he was the one, my Orpheus, even if it meant going down into hell for half the year.

MISTRESS   Look, I am not breaking up your marriage and I don't intend to . . . I am his mistress and I know the rules.

WIFE   You and your ilk are a pox on married households . . . up our husbands' asses, licking our husbands' asses . . . and we carry the can and smile and say, "Darling, shall we have Lourda O'Shaughnessy around for dinner?" She of the alabaster cleavage. And we smile and smile (*lower voice*) and get fat.

MISTRESS   He spends time with you . . . Christmas, Thanksgiving, anniversaries . . . values your advice about his work.

WIFE   He's washed up. He has a block. He can't deliver. It's different with actors, you can fake it . . . you have your (*pause*) repertoire of masks . . . that you put on and off at will . . . but a writer dons a mask at his peril. When he goes into solitary, he doesn't lie, Clarissa.

MISTRESS   (*scornful*)   What pearls of wisdom.

Wife picks up a vodka bottle off the dressing table.

WIFE   May I?

MISTRESS   Help yourself.

Wife drinks, savoring it.

WIFE   You went to Washington with him.

MISTRESS   Did I?

WIFE   I telephoned him at his hotel and the girl on the switchboard said he was out, so I tried later. She said, "Ma'am . . . you've been phoning all evening." I said: "No, that's his whore, that's his English whore that's been phoning all evening; can't you tell from our accents?"

MISTRESS Does he know what poisons you are dipped in?

Wife laughs lustily and takes Mistress's bare arm, strokes it.

WIFE I know you fancy women . . . I've checked you out
. . . you shared a suite in Philadelphia with a German girl
. . . the two of you stayed in that suite all day, all day until
it was time to go to the theater . . . she was your dresser was
she not . . . made you sheer dresses with tiny waists. Kiss
me . . . go on.

Wife kisses her.

WIFE (*passionate*) You'd like us both, Henry and me . . .
that's what you'd really like . . . Henry and me together . . .
because then you would not be an outsider . . . you would
be one of us . . . Henry watching me kissing you kissing
your cunt . . . Henry coming into you and into me and into
both . . . part of one another . . . that's what you really want
and that's what Henry wants . . . but he doesn't know it yet,
it will all just unfold . . . like seascape.

MISTRESS (*shrill, mirthless laugh*) That's *very* bizarre.

Wife brings her face close to Mistress's face.

WIFE What am I . . . a mind reader? . . . I know what you're
thinking . . . (*imitating an English accent*) Oh, Henry, please
come through that door and fuck us both and put an end to
all this torture and all this untruth and all this agony and all
this jealousy . . .

Mistress stands pushing Wife away.

*Wife touches Mistress's lips with her forefinger, then kisses her, a
longer kiss.*

WIFE (*cont.*) You're a piece of work, Clarissa.

Wife goes.

Mistress pours herself a drink and drinks in one gulp.

MISTRESS I just pictured her going home and saying, "She has a luscious mouth, your whore." For one awful second I yielded . . . I was unfaithful to him with his own wife.

SCENE SEVENTEEN

Daughter is tripping out and is standing, one foot on a chair, the other foot on the table, her arm stretched out calling a boy. Wife comes in but Daughter is unaware of anything except her trip. Disco music starts during her monologue as she creates a rock concert in her own mind and is the star of it. Strobe lighting. She is wearing a fur coat, inside out.

Daughter addresses imaginary audience.

DAUGHTER Zack . . . Zachary . . . I can't see you . . . you're hiding . . . hidey hidey (*whisper*) I'm wearing a see-through skirt with nothing on underneath . . . it seems we're going to the same party . . . you want dialogue . . . uh huh . . . that's tough . . . we're hooking up with Venus . . . you've got to take care of her . . . she gets catatonic after two lines (*She takes a tiny pill box and shakes it playfully.*) We get our goodies down the hill from the school at the pizza place . . . My mother would have a hissy fit. (*giggling*) We kind of know who to hit up . . . weird guy . . . Zack . . . you've got to get groovy . . . I mean university professor or not groovy is where it's at . . . enlightenment baby . . . Venus got blown away the first time . . . whiney about her belly flab. (*wooing*) To be perfectly profane about it Zack, it's good good shit. (*more alert*) You what . . . What . . . You're not coming? Never mind . . . it's not an issue . . . screw you. (*to her audience*) They've rented this huge space for the Homecoming Party . . . a bunch of us going . . . do you want to hear my dirty little secret . . . I'm performing . . . I'm the guest performance artist . . . cee-voo-play . . . (*rousing*) Ladies and gentlemen will you please welcome Miss . . . Brandy . . . Macready . . .

Deafening applause as Daughter starts to ad-lib from "I'll Take Care of You/It's a Man's World."

DAUGHTER (*cont.*) (*singing*)   I know what you're going through . . . and I want to take care of you.

Wife bursts into Daughter's space.

DAUGHTER (*cont.*)   Doobedoobedoo . . . doobedoobedoo . . . take care of you . . . we never have to worry . . . we never have to pine . . . you've got to trust me (*really loud*) trust me . . . trust me.

WIFE   Brandy.

Daughter ignores her and goes on with her solo.

DAUGHTER (*singing*)   Without a woman . . . without a girl . . . without a woman . . . (*speaking voice*) what town is it . . . (*singing*) without a woman without a woman.

Wife turns to Henry as if he is there.

WIFE (*loudly*)   You see what your fornicating has done to this family, this child.

Daughter takes off fur coat. She is wearing a skimpy slip.

DAUGHTER (*coy voice*)   Daddy . . . Daddy did I tell you I lost it . . . my cherry was popped . . . it was with Nathan . . . it was so (*searching*) nothing. I kept saying to him, "Is it over, is it over?" . . . now we do it wherever we get the chance . . . I'm very good at it . . . sex is not all it's cracked up to be but it's terrific not to be a virgin . . . virgin sucks. Sucks.

WIFE Jesus.

SCENE EIGHTEEN

MISTRESS I was asked to do a reading of his play—*The Winter Maze*. Very grand apartment. I played the older woman and Rebecca played my rival . . . There were two males, the nice guy and the shit. People sat on chairs and cushions, the cream, the cognoscenti . . . Pauline, on a high throne, very relaxed, the sphinx. Afterward people said such adoring things to him, people gloated over him, women were gushing, telling him how great he was, how deep, how moving. He had thrown me the odd bashful smile and then he came over and said, "What did you think?" and I said, "It was good Henry . . . but it doesn't cut the mustard." He was appalled. I knew it was curtains because I knew that above and beyond what the shits and the cognoscenti said, that he had his own doubts about it. People were watching us, nudging, and Pauline the sphinx was sitting up commanding. I tried to make amends. I tried to give him back to himself, but it was too late. He did something ugly. A poodle kept sniffing around his ankle, just would not abstain, and he called across and said, "Pauline, can you get this bitch off me?"

WIFE (*commandingly*) What's going on between you two?

MISTRESS He told her, said, "Clarissa thinks it doesn't cut the mustard."

WIFE (*going to her*) Oh really . . . and how do you come to that conclusion?

MISTRESS I can't lie to him . . . I don't lie to him about his work.

WIFE You think I do. You think he would have stayed with me all these years if I lied to him about what matters most to him in this world? You do us a disservice, my dear. Henry weighs every single word, a master jeweler, weighing his precious golds and his precious gems. Moreover, in case you think he stays with me because of my money you are also mistaken: Henry is a very independent man and I am not his purse. (*goes toward Mistress gloatingly*) You do know he does a real fine imitation of you for after-dinner guests. (*miming*) Your dying fall, the little flick of your wrists, your nasal sensitivity.

Mistress cowers.

Scene Nineteen

MISTRESS I had to come out of *As You Like It*.

WIFE Struck poor Celia across the cheek, a hard nasty blow.

MISTRESS Her acting was false, mincing . . . the director took . . .

WIFE . . . Took you aside, sat you down . . .

MISTRESS Said I needed time off. Time off . . . I who dreaded leisure. What to do. I walked . . .

WIFE She walked.

MISTRESS Got to know Manhattan . . . the smells, the heat belching up out of the grids . . . trumpet, trombone, the ghost hands of the homeless like twigs . . . people sitting on steps . . . talking to themselves.

WIFE   Crazy people . . . Thinking you would walk into him. In a bar. In that private club where he goes to play poker.

MISTRESS   There was this man on the pavement, very tall. Red beard, tartan rug, he sold cheap prints . . . the wounded orchids of Georgia O'Keeffe, wounded, spent. I spoke to him, asked if he ever cracked up. He looked at me. "Never." He was a mountain man and a Green Beret man . . . Plus I have God . . . Yes, that was his reply . . . I rang Rachel. I said, "Have you God, Rachel, do you feel the presence of God, are you enfolded in God's arms?"

WIFE   And Rachel told you—"You're having a breakdown, very soon they'll come for you and you'll be in a place upstate where the inmates are not allowed to lock their bedroom doors . . . bars on the windows . . ."

MISTRESS   Rachel must have telephoned him because one morning he was ringing my doorbell . . . Judge my disarray at him seeing me so unkempt . . . he bearing a large bunch of white roses . . .

WIFE   Not roses . . . definitely not roses . . .

MISTRESS   Let me say this, a man does not wish to see a woman on the verge of a breakdown . . . He had kept the car waiting . . . he was going to Washington to meet a senator . . . they're all opportunists. "I got laid by one," I said, harshly, too harshly, and he flinched and he said, "That's not very attractive, that's not like you," and I said, "I know, I know." He was in the doorway . . . and he said, "I did, do, and always will love you." I followed him out into the hall. It's a slow clunking lift. "Henry," I called.

"Clarissa," he called back. We had never said each other's names so tenderly, so . . . hopelessly . . . (*about to break*) They looked like roses . . .

WIFE   They were anemones . . . tall, white Japanese anemones . . .

MISTRESS   . . . and in the starlight they seemed to . . . blanch . . . (*suddenly howling*) HELP . . . HELP.

SCENE TWENTY

WIFE   My new therapist was tough . . . we did things called visualization and interaction. She started by making me roll bits of paper into snowballs and pelt them at her. Soon we got on to Henry, what I would like to do to him. For one instant I thought, This is absurd, this is dumb, and then she told me to take his clothes off and stand him in the dock, the bastard. She asked me what I wanted to do with his penis . . . what was the first thing I would do to his penis? "Cut it off," I said. And having cut it off she asked me what I wanted to do next. I hesitated. I thought we'd gone far enough. But no, she goaded me. She said, "Do you want to eat it, suck it, cut it up, or wear it." So we imagined me wearing it and she made me walk around the room, swagger. She said, "Have you ever had a woman? . . . being with a woman would get rid of some of your jealousy." And I said, "I'm getting rather fond of my jealousy . . ." and she made a note of that.

She moves downstage.

WIFE (*cont.*)   I came out of there and wrote him a letter. I said I would share him with her . . . Mailed it on the corner of

Fifty-eighth Street . . . opposite a luggage shop. Two
mornings later, it arrived, he read it, folded it, and put it in
his shirt pocket. He just shook his head and I realized that
we were each in a trap, and I thought, How will it end,
how will it end—one of us will indoubtedly be squeezed to
death in that trap. "Did Brandy get fitted with a coil," he
asked. "How do I know. She's a liar, and moreover, she
shoplifts." Shoplifts!

SCENE TWENTY-ONE

Wife and Mistress are reading an identical book.

MISTRESS I love this story . . . it was about a woman who
sleepwalked . . .

WIFE . . . Mrs. Rheinhardt.

MISTRESS At first she was rather timid and only ventured
into her own rose garden but then she got bolder, more
adventurous. One night she walked with a little son whom
she did not have and they went a long way into the
countryside and all of a sudden . . .

WIFE (*taking up the story*) They knelt down and began to
scrape the rich red earth for treasure that they knew was
there and they found . . .

MISTRESS (*joyous*) A latchkey. A talisman.

WIFE (*storytelling voice*) That night Mrs. Rheinhardt dreamt
that she was not in the country but back in London . . .
prowling about . . . and on her sleepwalk she came to a
mews house, number ten, with a big tub of flowers outside,
and she rummaged in the clay and found the key . . .

MISTRESS   . . . the same key as in her dream and she let herself in and there in the bedroom was her husband . . . waiting . . .

WIFE (*loud whisper*)   To be unfaithful with her. To ravish her. Those clandestine orgies went on and on in her sleep . . . then one day . . .

MISTRESS   . . . Mrs. Rheinhardt went to her husband's gallery on Bond Street . . . he'd gone out but his diary was on his desk, open, and there was the address of the mews house, number ten, penciled in, three, four times a week.

WIFE   She took a taxi and found the key and let herself in. The kitchen was minute . . . there was a pan in which an omelette had been cooked.

MISTRESS   Three eggshells . . .

WIFE   . . . two brown and one white . . . the fat was still warm in the pan.

MISTRESS   She stood at the bottom of the stairs and then (*triumphant*) she crept away, because it was clear to her that Mr. Rheinhardt went by day just as . . .

WIFE   . . . she went by night because they were on different tangents . . . but one day or one night they would come together . . .

MISTRESS   . . . arrive at the same time to the house of their dreams and up the stairs to the four-poster bed.

She gets up and goes to her own area.

Scene Twenty-two

MISTRESS (*happy*) The phone rang very early. My replacement had fallen and broken her shoulder and they asked me if I would consider coming back! Would I consider coming back! Friends said there was something different about my acting—scarier. (*softer voice*) Henry thought so too, and he knew why. I didn't have his child, I didn't have him in the fullest sense of the word, but we'd grown closer . . . we'd come through our black season.

WIFE (*overcheerful*) Clarissa, let's bury the hatchet. Come to dinner.

MISTRESS He would shout in his sleep and sit up . . . a nightmare. We were all on holiday, on someone's yacht and we, the women, were drowning and he couldn't save us, couldn't save all three of us and I said "Darling, we won't all be together on someone's yacht" and we'd hold each other and he'd say "Promise that you will always come to me in moonlight" and I promised, because that was how it had to be.

WIFE Monday, seven thirty, informal.

Scene Twenty-three

Mistress picks up her fringed shawl and allows it to trail across the floor as she goes.

Wife's area a sea of lighted candles. Wife has her hair pinned up and is wearing an apron; a picture of domesticity.

MISTRESS How . . . lovely; you've gone to such trouble.

WIFE I love going to trouble . . . a homebody . . . and guess what we're having?

MISTRESS   *Poulet roti.*

Wife shakes her head.

MISTRESS   *Poisson an vin blanc.*

Wife shakes her head even more, teasingly.

MISTRESS (*less sure of herself*)   *Caneton à l'orange.*

WIFE   Go on.

MISTRESS   Tripe.

WIFE   Truffles.

MISTRESS   Truffles! How extravagant.

WIFE   You look well . . . rested.

MISTRESS   I don't feel rested.

WIFE   Do you sleep on your face or on your back?

MISTRESS   It depends.

WIFE   I sleep on my face and I waken all swollen and pudgy.

Over her last speech, Wife has brought a tiny plate of truffles and toothpicks.

They both sit. Wife takes one. Mistress hesitates.

WIFE (*cont.*)   Come on . . . dig in . . . no need to stand on ceremony here.

Wife picks up a cookbook.

WIFE (*cont.*)   The truffle appears to be one of the original secrets of the universe. How does it get into the ground? Why should such diverse creatures as pregnant pigs and psychic dogs be the exclusive hounds for finding them?

(*more seductive*) The fragrance of truffles is impossible to explain—a truffle smells like . . . a truffle. But beyond its perfume the truffle has a visual quality which adds to its mystique. Black . . . flat . . . deep. The black punctuation of the truffle making a statement. (*consults cookbook*) The pig has a most keen sense of smell, without which it would never be able to find the treasure deep within the ground under the snows. Der Teufel—which means devil, Clarissa. (*pause*) Did Henry insist that you not have his child?

MISTRESS (*terse*) Yes.

WIFE You should have cheated . . . it would be a little person now . . . in its crib, gurgling away.

Mistress flinches—Wife holds a truffle to the Mistress's lips.

Mistress reluctantly takes it.

Mistress chews truffle, nervously.

WIFE You'd think they were poison.

MISTRESS Whereas, in fact, they are only little devils. (*looking around*) Have you sent Henry out, for this fest?

WIFE Didn't have to . . . he's gone.

MISTRESS (*thrown*) Gone?

WIFE To Ireland . . .

MISTRESS (*shocked*) No.

WIFE Across the ocean . . . (*half singing*) Oh little was my notion as I sailed across the ocean . . . (*speaking*) We went there, to Connemara, as you know, at Christmas, which was also our anniversary. We walked all day across flat, stone, misted country . . .

MISTRESS (*cutting in*)   Yes, he described it in his letters, the rain, the mist, the light, the people.

WIFE (*cutting in*)   At night we went to the local pub. There was a beautiful young girl, long auburn hair, shy, mysterious. On the last night she struck. Outside the window we could hear singing . . . quite ethereal . . . haunting . . . gave us goose pimples. Henry opened the window, it was the auburn girl, her hair all wet, like a fairy queen, and he just took her arm and brought her in. I knew that she had gone out there and sang for that very purpose, for Henry to open the window and bring her in. Quite a coup . . . They have corresponded. She sent him the words of songs . . . those fucking heartbreaking songs that got to him; she beckoned . . . and he went.

MISTRESS   You mean, you let him go . . . you didn't try to stop him? (*sharp*) Didn't slit your wrists?

WIFE   On the contrary, I helped him pack . . . put his warm sweaters in and his shoe trees—he's very fussy about his shoe trees . . .

MISTRESS   Why so considerate?

WIFE   She provides a new name, a new face, a new bed, sad songs . . . breaking the spell of you.

MISTRESS   Monster.

WIFE   Yes, you have made me so . . . but, as things stand . . .

MISTRESS (*cutting in sharp*)   As things stand . . .

Over the next speeches is the sound of the sea starting low then rising, louder louder, intercut with the singing of the AUBURN GIRL.

AUBURN GIRL (*offstage*) My young love said to me
My father won't mind
And my mother won't slight you
For your lack of kind.

WIFE (*exalting*) It couldn't be better . . . Back to his roots . . .
The old stories that his father taught him as a child, the
legends, there, in some cottage, a big fire, the smell of peat,
his sea nymph outside the window, or just come inside, into
the warmth . . . all the thrill of courtship.

Mistress rises and wraps herself inside her shawl, as protection.

Wife holds up a candle to usher her away.

A noise offstage of slamming door.

Daughter enters, disheveled, wearing a fur coat.

DAUGHTER Dear, darling, Mummy.

WIFE (*fending her off*) These overnight rave parties have to
stop . . . finito.

DAUGHTER Get your widows' weeds out, to look good for a
funeral.

WIFE She's crazy.

DAUGHTER Crazy yes . . . crazy, crazy, crazy. My father's
missing at sea.

MISTRESS (*aghast*) No. No.

DAUGHTER He went out in a blizzard in a little row boat.
He's missing five hours.

WIFE How you love to scare me . . . Daddy's gone a-
hunting. Daddy's gone a-missing.

DAUGHTER   They rang you but you were too busy clawing at her.

MISTRESS   Are they thinking missing . . . or is he washed ashore in some inlet.

WIFE (*abrupt*)   Whose talking missing . . . nobody. Moreover he's a brilliant sailor.

DAUGHTER   The fishermen warned them.

WIFE (*cutting in*)   Them?

DAUGHTER   There's a girl with him.

MISTRESS   Five hours. Five hours.

A scene of confusion follows, each doing something to defer the dreaded news.

Mistress relights the candle, holds it, murmuring to it, a prayer.

Daughter speaks to her cell phone . . . imploring it to ring.

WIFE   He's not dead Brandy . . . I would know . . . feel my pulse (*impatient*). *Feel* it.

DAUGHTER   You drove him to this.

WIFE   He wanted to go . . . a little dalliance.

DAUGHTER (*to phone*)   Don't die Daddy . . . don't, don't die.

WIFE   Cut it out Brandy.

DAUGHTER   I heard you the night before he left . . . shouting, screaming. What did you threaten him with—a bloodbath . . . you me and him or her? You would have done anything to split them up.

WIFE   Hold your tongue . . . these people have made you morbid.

DAUGHTER   These people live there and they know . . . they know the worst.

MISTRESS (*to daughter*)   Who called you . . . a doctor?

DAUGHTER   A priest. A brother of the girl . . . he said he would have stopped but he was saying mass . . . she was in love with the sea . . . the sea was calling to her and Daddy . . . she heard voices.

MISTRESS   She's snared him.

WIFE   She's sick. I must talk to this priest.

DAUGHTER   You can't . . . he's gone down to the sea shore . . . they're saying rosaries.

WIFE   Why aren't they out in lifeboats finding him?

DAUGHTER   They were . . . they gave up.

Auburn Girl singing offstage, her voice clear, enchanted and ghostly.

Wife speaks over the song to shut it out.

AUBURN GIRL (*offstage*)
My dead love came in
He came in so sweetly
His feet made no din
And this he did say
O it will not be long love
Till our wedding day

WIFE (*tenderly to Henry*)   My darling I will hold you in my arms, I will cradle you and hold you the way you hold me when I've been silly. I will never let you out of my sight again.

Wife exits to inner room.

MISTRESS Why did he go?

Daughter ignores the question.

MISTRESS Why?

DAUGHTER You know my father . . . anyone ask him a favor and he says yes. She pestered him. It was to launch some poetry magazine . . . a flying visit.

MISTRESS He will be back. We need him. We all need him so much.

Wife reenters carrying a black hat with veiling.

WIFE (*to Daughter*) Get ready . . . he'll want us there . . . to celebrate . . . to bring him home.

Wife looks in mirror as she puts on the hat.

Telephone rings offstage from inner room.

All three stand frozen, paralyzed.

Auburn Girl offstage in rasping urgent whisper, over the ringing phone.

AUBURN GIRL (*offstage*)
And the people they do be saying
No two were 'ere wed
But one had a sorrow
That never was said

Wife opens her mouth to speak but can't, no words come. She staggers.

Daughter goes and holds her.

Mistress looks on, the perpetual outsider.

The phone still ringing offstage.

Lights slowly go down.

A silence.

SCENE TWENTY-FOUR

Lights.

Spotlight on each.

WIFE   My husband was a wonderful man and a great writer ... we were inseparable ... so much so, that, he left a novel unfinished and I have decided to carry on the torch ... it will be my hand but Henry's immortal words.

DAUGHTER   (*showing a tattoo on her collar bone*)   What do you think Daddy ... do you like it? I'm seeing Zachary now ... big time ... we've been dating for quite a while ... he's so wise, so different from all the other slobs ... being a scientist he knows about the origins of life and stuff and I feel I can talk to him, tell him things, things about us, about you and me, the fun we had.

MISTRESS   I know it seems crazy ... but ... there's this pigeon that comes on my balcony at all hours ... whitish with tan spots ... without a mate ... potters, potters about and I know, it's Henry ... I know it's Henry making sure things are okay ... keeping watch over me. (*quieter*) It folds its wings and settles down at night . . . Henry loved the night . . . the silence.

Mistress stops suddenly, turns and whistles softly.

The THREE stand very still.

CURTAIN

IPHIGENIA

Euripides was born near Athens between 485 and 480 BC and grew up during the years of Athenian recovery after the Persian Wars. His first play was presented in 455 BC and he wrote some hundred altogether. Nineteen survive—a greater number than those of Aeschylus and Sophocles combined—including *Electra, Hippolytos, Andromache, Ion, Alkestis* and *The Women of Troy*. A year or two before his death he left Athens to lie at the court of the King of Macedon, dying there in 406 BC.

INTRODUCTION

Euripides was the scourge of his native Athens, his plays regarded as seditious and corrupting. Born in exile, on the island of Salamis, in 480 BC, he died in exile in Macedonia in his mid-seventies. Accounts differ as to the nature of his death, but chief among them is the hearsay that he was set upon and torn to death by mad dogs or mad women who could not tolerate his depiction of them as passionate, avenging, and murderous. His plays shocked public opinion, offended the critics, and ensured that he was over-looked year after year in the state competitions, with Sophocles and Aeschylus sharing the laurels. Sophocles was a distinguished figure who enjoyed public prestige, and Aeschylus could boast of his prowess in the war against the invading Persians. Euripides, however, was marginalized even though, as an able-bodied young man, he would have had to serve in army and fleet since Athens was vulnerable to marauders from east and west.

His crimes were legion. He had questioned the prestige of the state, of pious honor and ancient injunctions, had portrayed the gods as vicious, merciless, sparring creatures who gave rein to violent, even insane passions. Medea, who sent a robe of burning poison to her rival and subsequently butchered her children, was a heroine whose deeds were a blight on enlightened Athens, and the official judges of the annual prize put it at the bottom of the list. Three and a half centuries later, the historian Aelian said the judges "were either ignorant, imbecilic philistines, or else bribed." Euripides' depiction of women led to scatological rumors such as that he had learned their abnormal tendencies and sexual misconduct from everyday experience, that his mother Clito was an illiterate quack dabbling in herbs, potions, and fortune-telling, moreover he was a cuckold, a bigamist, and a misogynist who lived in rancorous isolation in a cave. It says much for his inward spirit and dedication to his calling that he wrote over a hundred plays—nineteen of which are in existense—and that when he died in Macedonia, Sophocles, out of a mark of delayed homage for his great rival, made his chorus wear mourning for the evening performance.

Euripides is the dramatist, along with Shakespeare, who delved most deeply into the doings and passions of men and women. His dramas, while being political, religious, and philosophic, are also lasting myths in which the beauty and lamentation of his choruses are in direct contrast with the barbarity of his subjects. As with Shakespeare he found the existing stories and legends too good, too primal, to be abandoned and so he appropriated tales from Homeric times, rewrote them, transformed them, and made them a foil for his prodigious imagination so that they serve as staple and forerunner for all drama that came after him. Sophocles' characters can seem stiff, their language elaborate, but Euripides'—vacillating, egotistical, unbridled, and warring—are as timely now as when they were conceived in the fifth century before Christ.

Iphigenia in Aulis is the least performed of his plays, having been described by ongoing scholars as being picturesque, burlesque, and in the vein of "New Comedy." Nothing could be further from the truth. The story is glaringly stark—Agamemnon, head of an oligarchic army, who has lived for power and conquest, is asked to sacrifice that which he loves most, his daughter Iphigenia. He demurs but we know that the lust for glory will prevail and yet in Euripides' drama, each voice, each need, each nuance is beautifully and thoroughly rendered. Iphigenia is for the chop but at the moment when her little universe is shattered, when she realizes that she is being betrayed by both God and man, she pitches herself into an exalted mental realm, the realm of the martyr-mystic who is prepared to die but not to kill for her country. It is of course, as probably in the myth surrounding Joan of Arc, a heightened, histrionic moment which pitches its heroine in the ranks of the immortals. If one of the prerogatives of art is to catapult an audience from the base to the sublime, from the rotten to the unrotten, from the hating to the non-hating, then Iphigenia does that, but her sacrifice prefigures a more hideous fate. The catharsis is brief, as the grand mechanism of war and slaughter has been set in place. Clytemnestra, the mother, helpless to avert her daughter's death, becomes an avenging fiend and ten years hence, when Agamemnon, victorious from Troy, will return with his Trojan concubine, the crazed prophetess Cassandra, he will meet a gory end at the hands of Clytemnestra and her paramour Aegisthus.

After his death in 408 BC three plays by Euripides were found—*Iphigenia in Aulis, Alcmaeon,* and *The Bacchanals* and were put on the stage by his son, Euripides III. *Iphigenia* was incomplete and finished by another hand. The other hand is what gives the play as we know it a false and substanseless ending. At the very last moment the sacrifice is aborted, Iphigenia whisked away and a deer put lying on the ground, the altar sprinkled with the necessary blood. It seems unthinkable that an artist of Euripides' unflinching integrity, with a depth and mercilessness of sensibility, would soften his powerful story for public palliation.

History has righted his standing. The Latin poets Virgil, Horace, and Ovid all acknowledged their debt to him, Plutarch would boast that he knew the plays by heart, and Goëthe devoted himself to reconstructing several of his plays from fragments. He now is recognized as the greatest of that triad of Athenian giants and even his fellow countryman Aristotle, after much carping, crowned him "that most tragic of poets."

Edna O'Brien
January 2003

For Michael Straughan who brought it to light

Iphigenia premiered at the Crucible Theatre, Sheffield on February 5, 2003. The cast was as follows:

WITCH/NURSE   Joanna Bacon

CALCHAS/MENELAUS   John Marquez

OLD MAN   Jack Carr

AGAMEMNON   Lloyd Owen

SIXTH GIRL   Charlotte Randle

IPHIGENIA   Lisa Dillon

CLYTEMNESTRA   Susan Brown

MESSENGER   Dominic Charles-Rouse

ACHILLES   Ben Price

CHORUS (Girls, Soldiers)	Kristin Atherton
	Olivia Bliss
	Veejay Kaur
	Francesca Larkin
	Charlotte Mills
	Kitty Randle
	Stacey Simpson
	Rachael Sylvester
	Andrew Hawley
	Martin Ware

Director   Anna Mackmin

Designer   Hayden Griffen

Lighting   Oliver Fenwick

Composers   Ben Ellin, Terry Davies

Sound Designer   Huw Williams

Choreographer   Scarlett Mackmin

A night scene, windless, hushed.

A starlit sky.

A high wall with ladders.

WITCH   Great Zeus stopped the winds and why. He sends winds to other men's expeditions, winds of sorrow, winds of hardship, winds to set sail, winds to drop sail, and winds of waiting but here upon the black and blasted straits of Aulis he sends no winds and an angry fleet keep asking why are we waiting, why is King Agamemnon hiding from us in his tent—because, because King Agamemnon, marshall of the fleet, made a vow to the goddess, Artemis of the sacred grove, a promise that he reneged on. Disastrous calm has driven him to augury, to Calchas the prophet who scans the flight of birds.

Spotlight on CALCHAS *the prophet.*

On the opposite side AGAMEMNON *emerges from his tent.*

The WITCH *hides under the wall to listen.*

CALCHAS   King Agamemnon—to Artemis, goddess of the moon, you vowed that you would sacrifice the most beautiful you knew. You shall not unmoor your ships until you pay your dues. Your wife Clytemnestra has a child Iphigenia who in all the radiance of young beauty has been selected by the goddess Artemis to be offered in sacrifice in order that the Greek ships can leave these narrow straits for the towers and battlements of Troy. Then and only then will amorous Helen be restored to her husband Menelaus, Troy in ashes, her nobles slaughtered, her women slave women, to bring home here to Argos and plentitude of spoils.

AGAMEMNON   My daughter, the jewel of my heart . . . no and no and no again.

CALCHAS   Her mother Clytemnestra must bring her here, intended as a bride for swift-footed Achilles, son of goddess Thetis, nurtured in the watery waves.

AGAMEMNON   You think I would deceive my wife and child.

CALCHAS   The gods think it.

AGAMEMNON   Be gone, you old werewolf.

CALCHAS   Your daughter's death ensures victory for Greece.

AGAMEMNON   Unspeakable . . . unthinkable . . .

CALCHAS   In time of war, unspeakable, unthinkable things are done. For the sake of the gods and for our land thus blasted with misfortune, send for her at once and sacrifice her on the altar of divinity.

AGAMEMNON   Who else have you spoken to of this hatching?

CALCHAS   Your brother Menelaus and Odysseus of the House of Athens. The goddess Artemis, lovely lady of the woodland and the forest, is growing impatient and your men wrathful at such long waiting.

AGAMEMNON   I will not do it.

CALCHAS   It will be done.

Calchas goes.

Agamemnon stands. When he turns, the Witch is in front of him.

WITCH   Hail, Agamemnon, the sacker of cities . . . the child shall have garlands put upon her head and sprinklings of lustral water. She comes to nourish with the drops of flowing blood the altar of the divine goddess from her own throat, her lovely body's throat. And grant that Agamemnon may wreathe the Hellene lances with a crown of fame and his own brows with the imperishable glory.

Agamemnon goes.

An OLD MAN *who has overheard pulls himself up from under the wall.*

OLD MAN   Dark. Darkness. The story goes of how Atreus, father of Agamemnon, had his brother's children foully and horribly slain, then boiled and served up at a banquet, all this, so that his own progeny, so that Agamemnon might rule. No one is safe. A curse is a curse. I was given as a young man with his wife Clytemnestra in all her dazzlement. I saw so much, too much. Oh, the passions, the passions; yet from great houses both were sprung.

Five wild YOUNG GIRLS *rush in, drenched, laughing.*

GIRL ONE   We have come through the pouring waters to see the long ships, the chariots, the dappled horses, and the spear men delighting in the throw of the discus.

GIRL TWO   Odysseus, son of Laertes, the chieftain Adrastus, earth-born Leitus, raging Menelaus that . . .

GIRL THREE   . . . lost Helen to Paris the herdsman, on the mount of Ida, lured her away he did with his waxen barbarian pipe and took her to Troy.

GIRL TWO   And Achilles, a marvel to mortals.

GIRL ONE   To glut our women's eyes.

OLD MAN   Where are your husbands?

GIRL ONE   At home.

GIRL THREE   They take their pleasure at the draughts board.

They start to climb the ladders.

OLD MAN   Harlots. Harlots.

Agamemnon comes out holding a book-shaped pine tablet.

AGAMEMNON   Gone. Gone is every hope I had of sweetness.

He signals to a Messenger.

AGAMEMNON   Take this to my wife. Give it into her own hands. Answer no questions. Tell her to do as I command. They are awaited here and she is to bring the dowry gifts for Iphigenia to be married to Achilles. Go. Go.

The Messenger goes.

OLD MAN   My master, the will of the gods has swerved against you.

AGAMEMNON   And made me wretched.

OLD MAN   A king is a mortal too. Power is power, but close neighbor to grief.

AGAMEMNON   What would you do if it were your daughter?

OLD MAN   My tongue dare not answer that. A brave deed, yet a fearsome one. The child will need to pray at the shrines along the way.

AGAMEMNON (*gravely*)   She will.

The Old Man goes.

A SIXTH GIRL *enters.*

AGAMEMNON (*to the constellations*)   What star are you and you and you? Do you shine into my child's bedroom where she sleeps innocent of all that will befall her? Send her a dream, tell her not to come here, tell her in language that befits her unschooled ears.

He crosses to a single star.

AGAMEMNON (*cont.*)   And what star are you?

SIXTH GIRL   Sirius . . . still high in the heavens.

Agamemnon turns sharply.

AGAMEMNON   Who are you?

SIXTH GIRL   A stranger woman. Sirius . . . sailing near the seven Pleiads the sisters, seven in number, Electra, Maia, Taygete, Alcyone, Merope, Celaeno, Sterope, whom Orion pursued, but they fled before him and Zeus, pitying them, placed them in the heavens. Only six are ever seen . . . the seventh hides in the bosom of the sky.

AGAMEMNON   Come here for what?

SIXTH GIRL   For what I find.

AGAMEMNON   Where is your husband?

SIXTH GIRL   Dead. Killed in the first strike of the war . . . on a small boat . . . sent out to reconnoiter in answer to the command of raging Menelaus. Goaded to frenzy on account of losing Helen.

Iphigenia

AGAMEMNON A good husband?

SIXTH GIRL A soldier good and bad.

AGAMEMNON So you have heard of Helen.

SIXTH GIRL Of course. The legend of how young men went
as suitors to Sparta . . . all desiring her . . . each one
threatened to murder the other if he was successful, so
when Menelaus of the House of Atreus won her, he made a
pact with all the others that if she should ever be taken, they
would all band together and fight. But Paris with
Aphrodite's help put the dart of love into her on Ida's
mountain among the white heifers and brought her thence
to Troy. It is why we are at war and why the thousand ships
out there are manned for passage. They say that even old
Hector, the father of Paris, worships her . . . walks with her
in the palace halls, bowing and discoursing like a young
gallant.

AGAMEMNON But you would see her dead for your husband's
sake.

SIXTH GIRL I would not. I would curry favor with her and
verse myself in all her wiles. Women can learn marvelous
things from captivating women. I have told you my history
. . . tell me yours . . . away from the main fleet . . . here in
your own quarters . . . you must be high up.

AGAMEMNON Would you like me to say that I am?

SIXTH GIRL Of course.

AGAMEMNON That I am King?

SIXTH GIRL Of course . . . every woman desires a king.

AGAMEMNON Do they speak of King Agamemnon in your
village?

SIXTH GIRL Ah no. The women speak of Achilles, the handsomest of all the Achaeans, who races in full armor on sand and shingle, racing against a four-horse chariot, lap after lap until the horses fall down in defeat.

AGAMEMNON Which would you rather look on, Achilles or the King?

SIXTH GIRL It depends. It may be that the King is old and past his prime.

AGAMEMNON What if I said that I were King?

SIXTH GIRL You, him? I would fall at your feet. King Agamemnon, leader of the Armada . . . supreme maneuverer of ships . . . respected in heaven . . . worshipped on earth . . . born for greatness . . . for war . . . for love of women . . . O great one . . . far from home . . . no soft bed . . . to lay your limbs on . . . turning this way and that in the night . . . duties to weigh you down . . . do you not sometimes wish you were a common man?

AGAMEMNON I wish it now.

SIXTH GIRL So we are equals.

He picks her up. In that embrace they go.

Off-stage the sounds of very young girls singing and playing a noisy game.

Scene Two

Early morning.

IPHIGENIA*'s chamber, where she and five Girls (two of whom are her sisters) are having a pillow fight. They speak in a made-up*

73

inexplicable language, running in and out, the feathers from the pillows falling through the air.

A NURSE *comes in.*

NURSE   The Queen. The Queen.

They stop instantly.

CLYTEMNESTRA *enters.*

IPHIGENIA   We're sorry.

CLYTEMNESTRA   Sorry?

IPHIGENIA   We won't do it again . . . we got carried away.

CLYTEMNESTRA   Dress yourself.

IPHIGENIA   Oh, Mother . . . it's only fun.

CLYTEMNESTRA   Your father wishes you at Aulis. We are to leave immediately.

SISTER   We are!

CLYTEMNESTRA   Not you.

IPHIGENIA   I knew Father would miss me . . . every night just before I sleep I say to the brightest star—"Please tell the King that Iphigenia misses him and is very lonely in this big palace without him . . . tell him to come home."

CLYTEMNESTRA   Dress yourself.

IPHIGENIA   Mother . . . I would miss you almost as much. Did you not sleep . . . had you a bad dream?

CLYTEMNESTRA   You are to be married.

NURSE   Praise be to Zeus, Pelius, Hera, and Aphrodite.

CLYTEMNESTRA To Achilles of Thessaly.

IPHIGENIA Who is he?

NURSE Son of the goddess Thetis and a mortal father Peleus, nurtured in the watery waves of the sea.

IPHIGENIA Is it true, Mother?

CLYTEMNESTRA The letter says so.

IPHIGENIA Why has he chosen me . . . he's never seen me.

CLYTEMNESTRA You are a king's daughter . . . that is enough.

IPHIGENIA And I will take my stand in the dances and the nuptial feast . . . whirling round and round for three days and three nights . . . Achilles will be in his own tent and on the fourth morning he will be led to me and I will sit there veiled until my bridesmaid slowly lifts it and Achilles gazes into my eyes. I wonder what color eyes he has.

NURSE Sea eyes, no color and every color.

SISTER Can I come?

CLYTEMNESTRA No . . . Iphigenia and baby Orestes and I will travel . . . the rest of you remain here.

SISTER She gets everything.

CLYTEMNESTRA You will have a husband, in time.

SISTER I want him now.

NURSE Hush, child, hush . . . this is her hour.

Clytemnestra goes.

The Nurse unfolds a corset. Iphigenia lifts her arms for her nightgown to be taken off, the Nurse pulling tightly on the corset strings.

IPHIGENIA   Ouch. Ouch. I can't breathe . . .

SISTER   What does he look like?

Nurse continues dressing Iphigenia.

NURSE   He has a coat of arms made of gold, given him by his mother. The story is known throughout, in Lesbos, Tenedos, Chryses, and Cilla, in all Apollo's cities and Skyrus too, how the nereid who was his mother took him down as a baby to the River Styx and submerged him in the water to protect him from all injury and so he was except for the little heel which she had held him by . . . then fearing he might be killed in the wars she had him dressed as a girl and hid him in the palace of a king who was her friend, where he lived among the king's daughters, but, one day a peddler came in to the palace forecourt with a tray of trinkets, ribbons, and scarves plus a spear and a shield and while all the girls loved the fallals, Achilles picked up the spear and the peddler, who was really the scheming Odysseus dressed in rags, saw the young boy's excitement and had a servant shout out an alarm to say the palace was under attack, whereupon Achilles tore off his woman's clothing and rushed to defend the gates and so Odysseus knew he had come to the right palace and Achilles was recruited into the Greek army, given noble rank and a vast host to command.

IPHIGENIA   He might change his mind when he sees me.

NURSE   Fate, my little one . . . the tiny threads of fate from heaven's loom, ordained this . . . This.

GIRL   What else, nurse?

NURSE   They say, that at the sight of him hearts are transformed.

GIRL How?

NURSE I daren't say.

IPHIGENIA How?

NURSE I lack the words, child.

GIRL What else?

NURSE His taste is to be solitary . . . he only shows himself for the tournaments and the championships and he always wins, being half a god.

IPHIGENIA Will you miss me?

NURSE More than I would my own children. The night you were born a rayon of gold shot across the sky, my name was the first name you said . . . not your noble mother Clytemnestra and not your noble father Agamemnon.

Sister One has taken out a veil yards long, is winding it around herself, both showing off and treading on it.

The Nurse rushes and takes it back.

NURSE You mustn't tear it . . . it's her wedding veil . . . it's sacred.

SISTER ONE Achilles might prefer me to her.

GIRL ONE You're jealous.

SISTER ONE It's you that said she was a sly one coaxing the Queen.

GIRL ONE I did not.

Iphigenia lets out a cry—her menstrual blood has started to flow, running down her legs.

SISTER ONE   Oh, look. Look.

NURSE   Sweet Iphigenia . . . sweetest Iphigenia . . . you
mustn't cry . . . this husband of yours has secured the rarest
prize . . . a girl just become a woman . . . a treasure.

*The Nurse rocks Iphigenia in her arms and sings a soft lullaby as she
leads her away.*

*The Girls lie on the floor on their bellies and one starts a pre-wedding
hymn, gradually the others join in and slowly with balletic precision
they make their way on their bellies along the stage and off.*

Change of light.

Two CHORUS GIRLS *enter.*

CHORUS GIRL ONE
   I passed along by the grove of Artemis
   Whose shrine is in the hollow of the hill.
   Shelter of Leto's travail
   Soft tossed palms
   The sweet laurel and silver swill of olive
   The earth red-hued, stained
   From much sacrifice.
   Overhearing that
   I would rather not speak of.

CHORUS GIRL TWO
   The Danaan warriors
   The oared ships of the Argives
   The fleet of Ajax
   The breezes soon
   To fill the sails
   To plough the unfriendly sea

To the walls of Troy
For the greatness of war is great.

SIXTH GIRL   Caring nothing for sacrifice.

SCENE THREE

The sound of men shouting, disputing, off-stage on the other side of the wall.

Sixth Girl is by a little brazier where she is boiling eggs in a long narrow saucepan.

Agamemnon emerges.

Sixth Girl takes boiled eggs from the saucepan, haws on them and cracks them on the ground. She offers one to Agamemnon, who eats it with relish.

AGAMEMNON   This . . . husband . . . of yours?

SIXTH GIRL   What about him?

AGAMEMNON   What about him . . . did you give him boiled eggs?

SIXTH GIRL   Sometimes . . . if we had any . . . The morning he left I did because he was on a grand expedition.

AGAMEMNON   And now, you're giving me boiled eggs . . . is that a . . . (*Instead of the word he traces her lips.*) Little serpent.

She starts to dance. He joins her in the dance but is not as carefree with the steps as she. She darts up the ladder.

She peers over the wall and looks down, then turns back.

SIXTH GIRL   These soldiers of yours . . . they're mad . . . they want to kill kill kill.

AGAMEMNON   I cannot stop them.

SIXTH GIRL   If you cannot, who can?

AGAMEMNON   I play the role expected of me.

SIXTH GIRL   O . . . King.

Agamemnon turns away, sits, and starts writing on the tablet.

SIXTH GIRL   Are you writing to me?

AGAMEMNON   No. (*pause*) To my daughter.

SIXTH GIRL   Is she beautiful?

AGAMEMNON   Yes.

Sixth Girl squats and stares directly at him.

SIXTH GIRL   Teach me the ways of the court . . . how to dance and be a lady.

AGAMEMNON   There is no time.

SIXTH GIRL   Don't send me home . . . there is no one there for me . . . Only rock and goats.

AGAMEMNON   You can't stay here . . . it's too dangerous . . . my men spy and gossip and would make trouble for us.

SIXTH GIRL   I will find a hole where I can hide and sometimes you will send for me.

AGAMEMNON   What makes you so sure that I will send for you?

SIXTH GIRL   Because the blood wills it.

He kisses her. She goes.

SIXTH GIRL (*cont.*)   A king. A king.

Agamemnon goes back to his letter.

Old Man comes in.

OLD MAN   A father again . . . you have kindled your heart.

AGAMEMNON   Sshhh . . . these walls have ears.

OLD MAN   You can trust me . . . I am a faithful friend.

AGAMEMNON   Find me a messenger.

OLD MAN   My son . . . the fastest boy in all of Argos.

AGAMEMNON   When you give it to him, tell him to learn it
   by heart in case he is set upon by thieves.

OLD MAN   Teach it to me, master . . . we do not have your
   learning.

AGAMEMNON   I send you this tablet, O daughter of Leda.
      In lieu of the former.
      Do not come to Aulis with the girl.
      The wedding celebrations are no longer.
      We shall feast our daughter's wedding another time.

*The Old Man murmurs it after him then hides the tablet under his
jacket.*

AGAMEMNON (*cont.*)   When he comes to a fork in the road,
   tell him to look in all directions in case they have already set
   out. If so, tell him to turn the carriage, the horses toward
   Atreus, to pilot them hence. Speed, speed.

Agamemnon goes.

WITCH (*from her bastion*)   The gods are not fooled. Upon the
   battlements of Troy and around its walls the Trojan guard
   now stand, but soon from over the sea the goodly ships of

Argos will draw into the channels of Simois to wreak slaughter. When Agamemnon has cut the head of Paris from his neck and has overturned that city there will be gnashing and tears among the maidens and wives. Lydian ladies in their golden robes cursing Helen, child of the long-necked swan, cause of all their disasters.

A Man shouting offstage. Hearing it the Witch hides herself once again as MENELAUS *pushes the Old Man onstage.*

OLD MAN My master will make you pay for this.

MENELAUS Traitor. Lackey.

OLD MAN I serve Agamemnon and none other . . . unbind me.

MENELAUS I should bloody you here and now.

Agamemnon appears.

OLD MAN Master. He snatched the letter from my hand as I walked to my son's hut . . . broke the seal and read it like a thief.

MENELAUS Oh, brother.

AGAMEMNON Hand it over.

MENELAUS Not before I show it to my comrades.

AGAMEMNON I am in command . . . I rule the army . . . I give orders.

MENELAUS Rule! You are ready to ditch them for your own crooked ends.

Agamemnon grabs the wooden tablet and smashes it in rage.

MENELAUS *(cont.)* They should see you now in dread and shame, trying to cover your tracks . . . remember how eager you were to curry favor, to be their commander . . .

Iphigenia

clasping every hand, keeping open house for every citizen to visit you . . . high and low all welcome.

AGAMEMNON And still are.

MENELAUS Phfff. You hide behind walls . . . you are seldom seen . . . when trouble started you showed yourself a man of straw . . . your ships were grounded and what solution did you arrive at—disband the army . . . send them home and only then did you come to me pleading, "What am I to do? What am I to do?," and when I suggested Calchas the prophet you rejoiced and when he told you the ships would sail if your daughter would be sacrificed you agreed after a few fatherly tears and sent a letter and slept on it and sent another—traitor, coward. The Trojan barbarians will not be assailed for the very simple expedient of you and your daughter's happiness. You are not a king.

AGAMEMNON Nor you a brother.

MENELAUS A weakling.

AGAMEMNON You call me that but what are you—a cuckold, a husband unable to keep his wife . . . something I am not charged with . . . no woman makes me wanting in the eyes of the world. You crave Helen back for lust or pride, or both, your so-called love of Greece, your great heroics a mere ploy that hides your basest need. I will not kill my child to fulfill your urges.

MENELAUS Nor will our plans be scuttled . . . a wind will blow us safe unto Troy's coast.

The young Messenger from Scene One rushes in.

MESSENGER My lord, Clytemnestra the Queen has just arrived. She was supported from her chariot holding the

baby Orestes lest she stumble. Soft maidenly arms reached
up to receive your daughter Iphigenia so that she would
not be frightened by so many strangers. They are now
bathing, the fillies let loose to drink and the army are
asking, asking, because a rumor has spread that the young
girl has come.

AGAMEMNON What rumor?

MESSENGER They gape to catch sight of the golden young
girl and ask why has Agamemnon sent for her, is it that he
misses her or is it that some marriage has been arranged for
her by Artemis, goddess of Aulis. They shout, let there be a
wedding to relieve the wretched waiting hours, let the pipes
sound in the tents, let the earth thud with dancing feet, they
are happy at the maiden's arrival . . . some see in it a
deliverance.

AGAMEMNON Run and see if they are still bathing or if they
are on their way toward the house.

The Messenger runs off.

AGAMEMNON (*cont.*) I am undone. (*to Menelaus*) What shall I
say to my wife? How shall I receive her? What expression
shall I assume? And my little daughter? It is when she pleads
with me that I will break. Argument such as her mother
excels in, merely hardens my resolve, but pleading . . .
Iphigenia pleading, her trusting eyes, her innocence, no
father should be asked for this.

MENELAUS Give me your hand.

AGAMEMNON Take it. For you there is victory, for me a
compact with ruin . . .

MENELAUS By my father and yours, by Atreus who begot us,
by the gods and goddesses, I see the tears that drop from

your eyes and I am not your enemy. I withdraw the harsh
words I spoke. It is not right that you should suffer this
agony—I do not want your child to die. Am I to win
Helen back by losing my brother's loyalty—no. Or
sacrifice my brother's child—no. What has Iphigenia to do
with all this—nothing. Let us disband the army, let them
leave these bitter straits of Aulis, scatter their ships, and go
home. I say this out of love for a brother and a deeper
honor than winning back a faithless wife. I will search for
her myself and drag her back to our homeland by her
cursed hair.

AGAMEMNON I welcome your words as a loyal brother, but
make no mistake we have come to a point where necessity
dictates our misfortune. We must carry out this bestial
command.

MENELAUS Who is forcing it?

AGAMEMNON The army.

MENELAUS They do not know of it yet. Send her back . . .
go down to the fast-flowing stream and tell your wife the
marriage with Achilles was something you dreamed, a
father's folly for his child.

AGAMEMNON Calchas will tell.

MENELAUS Not if he is dead.

AGAMEMNON By whose hands?

MENELAUS Ours.

AGAMEMNON To kill a seer invites great disaster and
moreover Odysseus knows, that wily cur. Already I can see
him standing before the army telling them how I proved
false. He will carry them with him and for good measure

allow them to kill us all . . . you, me, and my entire family. Even if we escaped they would follow us, destroy our city, our palace with its immemorial walls, our household and our tribe. She shall be sacrificed.

MENELAUS When?

AGAMEMNON Immediately—while this madness reigns over me. One favor, keep my wife away until it is done.

Over their speech stones have been thrown from beyond the wall and mutinous voices heard.

AGAMEMNON *(cont.)* Put an end to their brawls. Tell them to save their murderous rage for the hosts of Troy . . . for we are presently to sail to that Phrygian land.

MENELAUS Oh, my poor brother . . . Oh, my poor king.

AGAMEMNON As a broken king I go to war.

Menelaus goes.

Agamemnon hits his head against the wall, again and again, violently.

A stone is thrown over which almost hits him. He picks it up, looks at it and throws it back

Women's voices offstage.

Agamemnon rushes into his tent.

Clytemnestra enters. She turns back to give instructions to a maid.

CLYTEMNESTRA Put the baby down . . . rock him . . . the journey has made him fidgety, and take the dower gifts and carry them into the house, lay them carefully.

Iphigenia runs in.

Agamemnon in soldier's attire emerges.

IPHIGENIA   Father, Father.

CLYTEMNESTRA   My most reverent king, we are come and
we are glad to come.

Screaming of the baby offstage.

Clytemnestra goes off. Iphigenia holds flowers.

IPHIGENIA   Smell. I picked them specially for you. When we
were leaving my sisters clung to me, they wanted to come.
You are strange, more than strange, what has happened, has
this war made you so distant, so cold.

AGAMEMNON   The war has not even begun. We are
paralyzed. The ships are stuck out there idle . . . no winds to
lift the sails.

IPHIGENIA   Blow the winds blow, ho the winds ho . . .
You're not happy to see us.

AGAMEMNON   Happy. Yes yes.

IPHIGENIA   Take away that frown, Father. You've been
separated from us too long and we from you. I've made this
huge embroidery for you . . . a lamb in a meadow. It has
twenty shades of gold . . . Guess how I got them . . . guess
guess, I followed the turning of the sun from dawn until
sunset. It hangs in the great hall, just as you come in. You
can't miss it. We were so lonely without you and little
Orestes does not know his father but guess what, I taught
him to say your name . . . he has eight words in all, eight
baby words and a lisp. There are tears in your eyes.

AGAMEMNON   The time is not good.

IPHIGENIA   Forget war . . . give it up . . . send the men away . . . come home with us . . .

AGAMEMNON   If I could I would.

IPHIGENIA   Where is Achilles? Is he in his tent waiting? What shall I say to him? What shall he say to me? Does he have a little beard? Is his voice from down here? . . . Is his armor really gold . . . Answer me, Father, answer me.

AGAMEMNON   There is no answer.

IPHIGENIA   I believe you're jealous . . . that's why you're sulking.

AGAMEMNON   Shut up.

Iphigenia looks at him appalled. He has never shouted at her before. She runs off.

CLYTEMNESTRA   You have made her cry . . . why such a mood, such shiftiness?

Agamemnon turns and climbs the ladder to escape. Clytemnestra follows and pulls him back.

CLYTEMNESTRA (*cont.*)   Of course you hate to lose her, but think what I feel . . . I too will feel the pangs when I lead her along the steps to the marriage grove. Yet marriage is a great thing and we should welcome it. Tell me his character.

AGAMEMNON   Reserved. He is quite reserved. Chiron, it is said, reared him under the sea waves so that he should not learn wickedness from men.

CLYTEMNESTRA   Excellent. So no fault is to be found in him.

AGAMEMNON   He sits apart from all the others . . . aloof.

CLYTEMNESTRA   It is good. It is very good . . . where does he come from . . . from which city of Thessaly?

AGAMEMNON   Phthia, by the River Apidanus.

CLYTEMNESTRA   Blessing on them both. Which day are they to be married?

AGAMEMNON   When the moon comes full round.

CLYTEMNESTRA   That is lucky.
   Where shall I make the wedding feasts for the women?

AGAMEMNON   Down on the shore. But better leave all that to me.

CLYTEMNESTRA   Why?

AGAMEMNON   Lady, you will do as I say.

CLYTEMNESTRA   I am used to doing what you say . . . in everything . . . have you forgotten? And you have not kissed me. Are you afraid your men will think you weak?

AGAMEMNON   Go back home and take little Orestes with you.

CLYTEMNESTRA   What! Be absent from my daughter's wedding! Who will raise the bridal torch, who will say the prayers, who will crown her?

AGAMEMNON   I will.

CLYTEMNESTRA   That is not the usual style. A mother does these things . . . it is her privilege.

AGAMEMNON   I do not want you mingling with this rabble of soldiers.

CLYTEMNESTRA   I shan't mingle . . . I shall be with my husband, in his tent, under his protection.

AGAMEMNON   Obey!

He grips both her hands to convey his resolve.

She starts to bite his hands to free her own; the bite is both erotic and determined.

CLYTEMNESTRA   Your wife has missed you. A mother loves her children but a wife hankers for her husband once they have been put down to sleep. And have you not felt the same absense?

AGAMEMNON   I am at war.

CLYTEMNESTRA   War. War. War. Why are men so enamored of war?

AGAMEMNON   Go and tell her that I am sorry . . . leave me to settle something that must be settled. Patience, Clytemnestra . . . patience.

CLYTEMNESTRA   Is there something . . . fatal?

AGAMEMNON   No, no.

Clytemnestra leaves.

AGAMEMNON *(cont.)*   And so I plot and weave and slither against her that I love so dearly.

He goes.

Clytemnestra enters.

On her way Sixth Girl passes under the wall—they exchange a look.

They both go.

Agamemnon comes out and goes to the ladder.

A huge stone is thrown and again he picks it up and throws it back.

He climbs the ladder.

Music swells the stage as a procession of Young Girls comes on slowly, chanting a wedding song. They circle the stage.

WITCH
>To the strains of the Lythian lotus pipe
>Daughters of Nereus gather
>To stamp their golden sandals
>On the earthen floor
>For the wedding of Achilles, son of Peleus
>His suit of gold mail
>A gift
>From his divine mother Thetis.
>Daughters of Nereus join to crown
>Iphigenia's tresses.
>Iphigenia, a young heifer undefiled,
>(*shrieks*) is for the knife.

The Young Girls go inside and the music continues within.

SCENE FOUR

Clytemnestra enters, goes in search of Agamemnon.

When she comes out, Sixth Girl is waiting for her.

SIXTH GIRL   May I speak with you.

CLYTEMNESTRA   Who are you?

SIXTH GIRL   A woman (*pause*) that befriends her sex.

CLYTEMNESTRA   Really! And follows the camp to pick the leavings.

SIXTH GIRL   My bed was cold. I lost a husband on account of Helen. Something is being kept hidden from you.

CLYTEMNESTRA   What?

SIXTH GIRL   Your daughter is to be sacrificed in order that they can hoist the sails and make war on Troy.

CLYTEMNESTRA   You rave.

SIXTH GIRL   Unhappy lady . . . you will wish you had let me into your confidence and opened that haughty heart of yours.

Sixth Girl goes.

ACHILLES *in full armor comes down the ladder.*

Clytemnestra draws aside.

ACHILLES   Agamemnon, captain of the army, Achilles stands before your door . . . the men grow fierce . . . they curse . . . their murmurs swell. "How long more, how long more for the voyage to Ilium. What does Agamemnon intend to do, send us home." Wreak shame on the House of Atreus and leave an army in perpetual desolation.

Over his speech the Old Man has come on from one side and Clytemnestra from the other.

CLYTEMNESTRA   Achilles, prince of greatness.

ACHILLES   How is this—a woman . . . So stately and so fair. Revered lady . . . this is no place for a woman, fenced in by an undisciplined mob.

CLYTEMNESTRA   I am Clytemnestra, wife of the King and mother of Iphigenia.
    Why do you run . . . join hands with me . . . as a happy prelude for the bridals.

Iphigenia

ACHILLES   Touch your hand! I could not face Agamemnon if I touched that which I have no right to.

CLYTEMNESTRA   I admire your constraint, Achilles, son of the sea, but you are to marry my daughter Iphigenia, so we are already joined are we not?

ACHILLES   Madam, you talk like a storybook.

CLYTEMNESTRA   So formal on the brink of wedlock. Why?

ACHILLES   Wedlock?

CLYTEMNESTRA   To Iphigenia.

ACHILLES   I have not courted your daughter Iphigenia and marriage is far from my mind. Ten thousand girls hunt for marriage with me, but I am a soldier first and last.

CLYTEMNESTRA   I am sorry if I have overstepped—I am mortified. I took you for my son—an empty hope. You say you are not marrying her, an evil omen for her, for all.

Clytemnestra goes to leave.

OLD MAN   Lady, I hold you dear. Your father pledged me to watch over you in danger.

CLYTEMNESTRA   Not now . . . That youth has irked me.

OLD MAN   With cause. Don't blame him.
    O Gods, save those I once saved. Save the seed of Agamemnon. A horrible deed is contrived, we are undone.

CLYTEMNESTRA   Riddles.

OLD MAN   The father that begat Iphigenia is going to kill her . . . to sacrifice her on the altar to Artemis.

CLYTEMNESTRA   You're out of your mind.

OLD MAN   It's what the girl from across the straits tried to tell you. All is prepared, the altar, the meal cakes, the cups for the blood . . . he will slit the child's throat with a sword before the sun goes down.

CLYTEMNESTRA   You are mad.

OLD MAN   No. The King is mad.

CLYTEMNESTRA   Why would he do this?

OLD MAN   Oracles. Oracles . . . so the army can sail to Troy and Helen be brought back restored to Menelaus.

CLYTEMNESTRA   How do you know?

OLD MAN   I was sent with a second letter to you, in lieu of the first, it said, "Do not come to Aulis, do not bring Iphigenia here." Menelaus met me and intercepted it . . . he is behind it . . . so is the prophet Calchas and crafty Odysseus . . . Achilles was a husband in name only, the marriage promise was a snare.

CLYTEMNESTRA   I think I see.

ACHILLES   I should not have spoken to you as I did. My pride was pricked. I am sometimes hasty.

CLYTEMNESTRA   As befits a warrior.

ACHILLES   Your husband used my name and fame for his own base ends.

CLYTEMNESTRA   Think how I feel, drawn in by his honeyed wooing, a wife of many years, this child is an angel, she thinks her father supreme above all.

ACHILLES   He will not succeed in this malevolent scheme.

CLYTEMNESTRA   I fear it is already commenced. He left here hurriedly, no doubt to confer with Calchas the prophet.

ACHILLES   Prophets serve their own interests, they say what suits the moment.

CLYTEMNESTRA   Yet they can wreak magic too.

ACHILLES   Let Calchas wreak good magic then.

CLYTEMNESTRA   I am at your mercy. Guide me.

ACHILLES   Act cunningly. When he returns draw him out as to what is weighing upon him, do it with your old sweetness, say you have observed his gloom, bring him round to a better mind.

CLYTEMNESTRA   And then?

ACHILLES   Together you will find a way to spirit her off to safety.

CLYTEMNESTRA   What if we are not together but more divided?

ACHILLES   As I live, I shall save the girl.

CLYTEMNESTRA   O prince of princes, can that be true?

ACHILLES   The army respect me, despite my young years. I will convene the generals, they are not fiends, they are not gutless knaves.

CLYTEMNESTRA   Would it not be better if you spoke with him in all your prestige?

ACHILLES   Not yet. My place in the army must not be compromised. Take the course I counsel.

CLYTEMNESTRA   If I fail . . .

ACHILLES   Then you may send for me.

CLYTEMNESTRA You are aware how cruel he can be, how ruthless?

ACHILLES I was not brought up to flinch in the face of danger. I no longer see him as my master, for I am his.

CLYTEMNESTRA For you I garlanded her, I brought her here for you. Let me ask you one last thing—see her and your heart will melt, so young, so shy, so modest, so full of trust.

ACHILLES Do not bring her into my sight—a soldier does not court the things that make him weak.

CLYTEMNESTRA You will save her from death?

ACHILLES I have said so.

Achilles goes up the ladder. Clytemnestra watches.

The music and revels from inside grow louder.

Agamemnon appears on the top rung of the ladder.

The Old Man goes.

Agamemnon comes down.

AGAMEMNON They are singing within.

CLYTEMNESTRA Indeed . . . singing *and* dancing.

AGAMEMNON They seem very merry.

CLYTEMNESTRA And you . . . you seem solemn . . . would it not help to unburden yourself . . . to let me know of this gravity.

AGAMEMNON Where do I begin. The yoke of circumstance . . . here in Aulis I am not a free man . . . a violent rage, a supernatural rage possesses them.

Iphigenia

CLYTEMNESTRA   And has infected you. You have a notion to kill your own daughter.

AGAMEMNON   Who said such a thing? Who dares accuse me of this?

CLYTEMNESTRA   It is written across your face. The moment we arrived I saw that some dreadful constraint was upon you . . . the way you twisted and turned and could not look in my eye or in hers.

AGAMEMNON   Whoever spread this rumor shall be mortally punished.

CLYTEMNESTRA   Isn't one death enough to contemplate in one day, your own daughter's at that. Who will draw the sword across her child's neck?

Echo of "Who will draw the sword across her child's neck" *twice.*

AGAMEMNON   I will.

CLYTEMNESTRA   Who will slit it?

Echo of "Who will slit it" *once.*

AGAMEMNON   I will.

CLYTEMNESTRA   Who will hold the cup for the . . . torrent of blood?

AGAMEMNON   I will.

CLYTEMNESTRA   The blade will fall from your hand.

AGAMEMNON   Others will raise it up.

CLYTEMNESTRA   Others. Lesser men. Menials. Stand up to them, show courage, or are you so eager to parade your scepter and play the general.

AGAMEMNON   I do not count her wise, a wife, who when her husband is on the rack goads him further. Think what I have been through, think of how I have suffered, tossed from love to duty and back again, like a puppet.

CLYTEMNESTRA   I will not let this happen.
Defy Artemis.

AGAMEMNON   Defy her and risk her greater wrath . . . murder for all of us . . . you, me, Iphigenia, the baby . . . . it is out of my hands, even though my hand will be the doer of it.

Clytemnestra realizes that he is serious and rounds on him now, striking him.

CLYTEMNESTRA   You killed the child I bore from Tantalus, you tore it from my breast and dashed it to the ground, murderer . . .

AGAMEMNON   A murderer's accomplice—you came with me, your tresses unbound.

CLYTEMNESTRA   I did it for my poor aged father's sake—he whom you tricked with your honeyed words, the way you tricked me.

AGAMEMNON   Sister of Helen, daughter of Leda, sisters in lust.

CLYTEMNESTRA   You dare lump me in with Helen! I grew temperate in Aphrodite's realm, a blameless wife toward you and your household . . . I bore you children . . . Iphigenia, her sisters, and little Orestes, who is in there now with her, two children believing themselves to be safe in their parents' quarters, under their parents' tutelage.

AGAMEMNON   From the moment I received the oracle I have been mad, mad. Phantom females dripping with blood visit me in my sleep.

CLYTEMNESTRA Huh. Phantom females.

AGAMEMNON I love my child as much and more than any father could.

CLYTEMNESTRA What prayers will you utter after she is dead. Do you think when you come home to Argos your other children will embrace you, your wife will welcome you back—God forbid it.

AGAMEMNON Be my companion in this . . . help me.

CLYTEMNESTRA Let Helen's daughter Hermione be sacrificed, it is only right, she too is young and fair, tell Menelaus to send for her and let her be swapped for our darling girl.

AGAMEMNON Iphigenia was named as being the most pure, the one marked for godhead.

CLYTEMNESTRA Then Achilles must save her.

AGAMEMNON Achilles must not know of this.

CLYTEMNESTRA He knows. He was here when the message was relayed to me, not by one . . . but by more than one . . . he smarted at being used as a foil . . . a mockery of his standing . . . but he gave me his word that Iphigenia will be saved.

AGAMEMNON Would that she could.

CLYTEMNESTRA Let us flee now, as a family, call the children. Let us outwit them . . . arrange for the carriage. Do it.

AGAMEMNON It's no use.

CLYTEMNESTRA You speak as if the deed is already done.

AGAMEMNON It is.

From his back pocket he takes out a bloodied knife and she screams repeatedly.

AGAMEMNON *(cont.)*   I slew a lamb in preparation.

Iphigenia runs out at hearing her mother's scream.

IPHIGENIA   Mother! Why are you screaming? Are you and father arguing . . . but why, I am so happy . . . be happy with me . . . . don't spoil it . . . I have been hearing about my husband . . . his feet are like the wind and he races on the shore against a four-horse chariot, lap after lap, day after day. O Mother, O Father, I thank you for giving me life, for being always so loving and so gentle with me . . . I thank you for Achilles, they say too that he sits alone, even at the feast, he is Achilles the unreachable and I shall have to humor him, the way I humor you . . . father.

CLYTEMNESTRA   Tell her.

AGAMEMNON   Iphigenia . . . child of my heart. I did not bring you here of my own free will, nor are you betrothed to Achilles.

IPHIGENIA   Why not?

CLYTEMNESTRA   Your father intends to sacrifice you to Artemis the goddess.

IPHIGENIA   What a tall story.

AGAMEMNON   The gods have willed it.

IPHIGENIA   I begin to go cold.

Agamemnon exits.

Girls from inside the house have come out to listen.

IPHIGENIA   Let's get Orestes and run away.

CLYTEMNESTRA   We can't . . . we are watched on every side. I
will have you escorted to Achilles' tent . . . to plead with him.

IPHIGENIA   No . . . no . . . the shame is too much . . . the
shame on him and on me.

CLYTEMNESTRA   Show him how you feel . . . reveal it . . .
give him the bait and he will take it . . . he is young, virile.

IPHIGENIA   I can't do it, Mother.

CLYTEMNESTRA   This is no time for delicacy.

IPHIGENIA   My father will save me.

CLYTEMNESTRA   Your father killed my first husband Tantalus
. . . the babe of that first husband he wrenched it from my
breast and smashed it to the ground. Pray that you do not
cause me a bitterer grief.

A PRAYING GIRL *comes on.*

Agamemnon returns.

IPHIGENIA   How far is Troy . . . I will come with you.

CLYTEMNESTRA   Let her hear it from your own lips . . . tell
her that she is to be slaughtered in order to bring Helen
back.

IPHIGENIA   I know nothing of Helen . . . I love life . . . why
would I have to die for her sake?

AGAMEMNON   Artemis wills it.

IPHIGENIA   Why would Artemis pick on me?

AGAMEMNON   On account of being ripe for beatitude.

IPHIGENIA   Beatitude.

Iphigenia crosses to the Praying Girl muttering the word "Beatitude."

Iphigenia

Praying Girl kneels and rings the bell repeatedly.

Witch starts to sway, working herself into a trance.

PRAYING GIRL
So gentle are you, Artemis the holy
So loving are you, to dewy youth to tender nursling.
The young of all that roam the meadow
Of all who live within the forest
You protect
Hear us, Artemis
Do not have your altar stained
With human blood.

Praying Girl waits and they all wait.

Sounds like thunderclaps offstage.

PRAYING GIRL (*cont.*)   Sshh. Sshh. The goddess speaks . . .

Witch tears open her coat to reveal her goddess attire.

Artemis speaks through the Witch.

ARTEMIS
Would that Paris had died
On the lonely mountain where he was left
Cast out to die on an oracle's command
Hapless, unmothered
Paris the shepherd lad, prince of Troy
Would that he had died
By the lakeside
By the nymph-haunted fountains
By the meadows, starry with roses
Would that he had perished
But no
Beauty's queen came

102

Child of the long-necked swan
The blame for all those troubles.
Iphigenia
Child without blemish
Blessed above all the maidens
Undo these wrongs.
The altar is well prepared
The blood of the lamb upon the pyre
Say your farewells
For it is time
For it is time
Swap your raiment
Revere the sacrifice
Not with wailing
But with prayer
When you have fulfilled your destiny
You shall be raised among the blessed
And our dear land will honor you for ever
For it is time
For it is time.

Iphigenia runs to her father.

IPHIGENIA   Save me.

AGAMEMNON   I can't.

CLYTEMNESTRA   Vile Helen, I curse you now in whosoever's
arms you bask, the swan's neck I hack with daggers, those
gray dreaming eyes I gouge from their sockets; or better
still, O daughters of Nereus, bring her here that I may maul
her with my own hands.

AGAMEMNON   A mother in name only, harken to the child
with soothing prayer.

O golden hair, what burden Phrygia's town has laid upon you.

IPHIGENIA   No, the Greeks my own people are doing it to me.

AGAMEMNON   That rage of my army is not against you, child, but a mad rage to sail to the barbarian land, to quash them and put an end to their rape of our women . . . Greek women . . . Greek wives . . . Greek daughters defiled. Greek men will not permit that most loathsome of crimes. It is not for Helen, not for Menelaus I sacrifice you, it is for Greece. She must be free. If it is in our power, yours and mine, to make her so, we must.

IPHIGENIA   It falls to me alone . . . without you.

AGAMEMNON   It does.

IPHIGENIA   If I had Orpheus' eloquence . . . the voice to charm the rocks . . . . if I could bewitch with words, I would bewitch now . . . but I only have tears and prayers . . . and these I offer . . . like a suppliant . . . O Father, I press against you now . . . this body of mine . . . which my mother bore . . . do not destroy me before my time . . . I love the light . . . do not despatch me down to the netherworld . . . hell is dark and creepy and I have no friends there . . . I am your child . . . I basked in your love . . . the little games we played . . . you would close the folding door and I would squeak squeak and you would come back in with sugar plums and put them under my pillow . . . you were never cross with me . . . never haughty . . . never the King . . . I could coax you out of your moods and when you grew a beard, I studied it . . . I counted the hairs, I pulled on it and clung to you as I cling to you now, my first and last and only hope. In your old age I will

welcome you into my own house with my own husband—
whoever he be—I will have children to lighten your weary
heart . . . look at me . . . give me a kiss . . . at least let me
have that as a memory of you . . . if am to . . . if I am to die.

SOLDIER *rushes in.*

SOLDIER   The anger of heaven is nothing to the anger of
men. They had heard that Achilles wanted to save the
young girl and they leaped upon him, seizing him by his
helmet, swung him from his feet and as the first stone was
thrown, a hail of stones were aimed at him to decapitate his
head from his neck.

Menelaus comes in during his speech.

SOLDIER (*cont.*)   They would have killed him but that
Odysseus said that even if Achilles had turned coward the
sacrifice would be performed and so a few of his men that
were loyal to him made a wall before him and took the
stones.

AGAMEMNON   Did his own guard not save him?

MENELAUS   They were the first to turn against him—they
called him lovesick because he pleaded for the girl.

Achilles is carried in in the arms of two bodyguards.

PRAYING GIRL   O healer Phoebus, make great Achilles well
again.

GIRL TWO   Thetis, come down and save your godly son.

*Iphigenia crosses and stands over him. She begins to take out the
stones from his wounds. This is the turning point for her.*

Soldiers have climbed on the far side of the wall, calling her name.

AGAMEMNON   Get Odysseus to fend them back . . . tell him that . . .

MENELAUS   Tell him what?

IPHIGENIA   I will die.
Let me save Hellas if that is what the gods want. What is one life compared with thousands. I will do it gloriously . . . I will put frightened thoughts out of my head.

ACHILLES   Shining one.

IPHIGENIA   Don't stir.

ACHILLES   I swore to save you.

IPHIGENIA   You will be my chariot on the path across . . .

ACHILLES   I will die with you.

IPHIGENIA   And fail Greece—no. You risked your life for me and that is everything.

ACHILLES   Iphigenia . . . Pure star of our destiny.

Clytemnestra slaps Iphigenia on the face to put sense into her.

IPHIGENIA   Mother, I am happy . . . and one must not love life too much.

CLYTEMNESTRA   Child's talk . . . babble . . . you do not know what this means.

IPHIGENIA   I do know (*pause*) it is the end for me. Achilles tried to save me, one against all, and now I am alone.

CLYTEMNESTRA   When the blade rips into your flesh you will cry for mercy.

IPHIGENIA   Pray that I don't. Pray that I draw courage from you and you from me, Mother. If we can't give each other courage, who else can? We have lived a long time since we set out from home, the horses so frisky, the morning so young. Do not cut your hair, Mother, and do not go into mourning . . . you have my sisters and little Orestes who will grow into a man.

OLD MAN Diverse are the natures of the mortals, she willing to die for valor and they willing to kill.

Clytemnestra in a last desperate attempt holds Iphigenia's face in her hands.

CLYTEMNESTRA Death is a fearful thing.

Iphigenia kisses her mother.

Agamemnon stands like someone in a trance.

AGAMEMNON There will be much adornment . . . she will be bathed in yellow oils, the tawny mountain honey will anoint her body . . . she shall rest upon the cenotaph; laurels, roses, and hyacinths all around her.

CLYTEMNESTRA The man has gone mad. He speaks as if it is a wedding feast.

IPHIGENIA O, poor Father. O, poor King.

CLYTEMNESTRA Man of stone.

AGAMEMNON In death I shall hold you dearer than in life.

Agamemnon embraces her.

Over that embrace the death ritual commences.

Menelaus takes a sword. Clytemnestra runs to grab it from him and risks her own hand to seize it. They fight over it.

MENELAUS Seize her.

Iphigenia

Two men lift Clytemnestra up and pull her backward as she screams. One puts his hand across her mouth to muzzle her.

MENELAUS   Discord between brothers must never be allowed to fester, we are our mother's sons. She too presides above the altar of Artemis, wishing us godspeed to Ilium.

Iphigenia is raised up and carried offstage toward the altar.

Agamemnon follows.

AGAMEMNON   Even now this heart breaks.

Menelaus gives Agamemnon the sword.

Death shrieks—all female.

The blood begins to drip.

That sound held for a moment.

A breeze gusts along the stage, raising the trampled feathers from Scene Two.

The men let go of Clytemnestra.

The death shrieks and music continue.

WITCH   Fortunes now attained . . . the glittering seat of Atreus awash with victory.

PRAYING GIRL (*coming out*)   The blood from her gashed throat matted the curls of her hair.

MENELAUS (*coming out*)   Wise men ride their luck; they seize the chance to be great, to win fame and honor.

As he climbs the ladder he shouts triumphantly to the men.

MENELAUS (*cont.*)   Hoist the sales . . . let the trumpets blare.

Agamemnon returns, a Girl pouring water over his bloodied hands. When they are washed he smells them and goes to Clytemnestra.

AGAMEMNON   Noble Queen.

Clytemnestra stands with a cold, still loathing.

CLYTEMNESTRA   Killed for a charm against the Thracian winds.

AGAMEMNON   Will you not kiss a king goodbye. (*pause*) A husband then . . . Farewell. It will be long before I address you again.

Agamemnon climbs the ladder—she does not watch.

Clytemnestra stands utterly still.

Sixth Girl wearing a veil stands a little away from her as if to ask her something.

GIRL ONE   There is no one left for her here.

CLYTEMNESTRA   She may follow us. Her cunning will serve some purpose.

Sixth Girl lifts the veil, bows and goes off.

Bloodied rain starts to fall and Clytemnestra is drenched in it.

The Young Girls rise vivified, climb on to the ladders, speaking the prophecy of the fate to come.

(*The lines are broken up and can be given as desired.*)

YOUNG GIRLS
What all men fear.
Gold and silver brought back in the Aegean ships.
The captive women of Troy.
Cassandra, daughter of Priam, Virgin of Apollo, chosen by

Lord Agamemnon to be his concubine.
In contempt of the gods and all pious feeling.
Brought back to the House of Atreus.
You will greet your war-torn husband with every appearance
of delight.
Unroll the purple carpet.
Lead him to the bathhouse.
When he steps out of the bath, eager for banquet, you will
come forward . . .
As if to wrap a towel about him but instead . . .
It is a net . . .
Entangled in it like a fish, Agamemnon will perish at the
hands of Aegisthus, son of Thysetes and corruptor of
your marriage bed.
The broad blade driven in to Agamemnon's garlanded
throat.
He falls on the silver-sided bath, his brain awhirl, in death
convulsion, his eyes staring in disbelief at you, at you his
queen.
Will add her hand to the hand of Aegisthus and drive the
blade clean home into your king's breast, exacting the full
price . . .
On the thirteenth day of Gamelian.
Not troubling to close his eyeballs and wiping the blood off
your hands, you will return to the feast, unafraid of
divine retribution.

CLYTEMNESTRA
Sweeter to me your words
Than heaven's raindrops
When the cornland buds.

Darkness.